HORSE FACTS

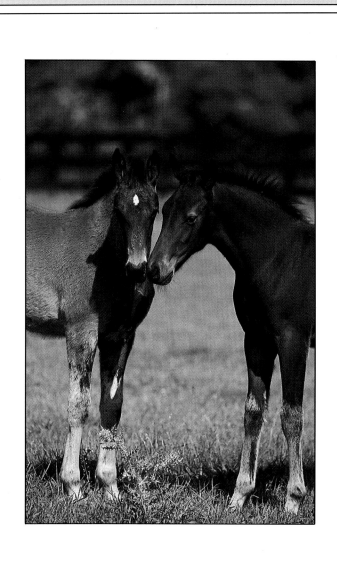

HORSE
FACTS

Susan McBane

and

Helen Douglas-Cooper

BARNES
&NOBLE
BOOKS
NEW YORK

A QUANTUM BOOK

This edition published by
Barnes & Noble, Inc.,
by arrangement with Quantum Books Ltd
1996 Barnes & Noble Books

ISBN 0-88029-559-7

M   10   9   8   7   6   5   4

This book was produced by
Quantum Books Ltd
6 Blundell Street
London N7 9BH

Senior Editor Cathy Meeus

Art Editor Anita Ruddell

Designer Hazel Edington

Illustrators Wayne Ford, John Francis, David Kemp,
Janos Marffy, QED

Picture Manager Joanna Wiese

Art Director Nick Buzzard

Publishing Director Janet Slingsby

Quarto would also like to thank the following for their
assistance: King and King, Karin Skånberg
Printed in Singapore by Star Standard Industries Pte. Ltd.

CONTENTS

Section 1
THE NATURE OF THE HORSE

Section 2
HORSE BREEDS

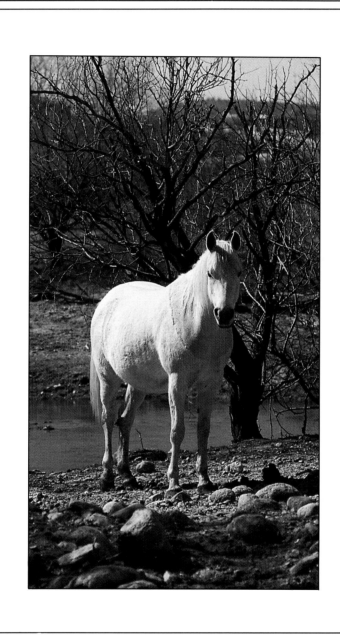

THE
NATURE
OF THE
HORSE

THE ORIGINS OF THE HORSE

THE EARLIEST HORSE ancestor, known as *Hyracotherium* (formerly as *Eohippus*), was discovered in North America from fossils about 50 million years old, and similar fossils have been found in Europe. It was a lamb-sized mammal with four toes on its front feet and three on its hind feet.

Strains of *Hyracotherium* existed from 50 to 38 million years ago. It was a forest and swamp-dwelling animal, grassy plains not yet having developed. It appeared first in North America, and later migrated from there across the land mass into Europe (the two were not at that time separated by the Atlantic ocean).

As the earth's climate changed, so did the vegetation. Parts of the earth became cooler and drier and grasses and open plains evolved; as this happened the early horse types became longer-legged and faster, and the number of toes was reduced to three all round. Two groups of three-toed horses emerged; browsers, who fed on leaves, and grazers, who fed on grasses. Browsers appeared first, but became extinct about 11 million years ago. Grazers, which appeared about 10 to 15 million years ago, were larger and longer-legged than browsers and were more efficient feeders. Some historians claim that Alexander the Great's charger, Bucephalus, had three toes on each leg, only the central one bearing weight, and that it was thus a throwback to a primeval form

Right: The Exmoor Pony is thought to have existed in south-western England since prehistoric times. It is believed to be descended from the original Celtic pony of western Europe. The breed has remained very pure and is thought to have changed little since primitive times.

Below: Eohippus (far left), also known as Hyracotherium, is one of the earliest equine ancestors. It lived around 50 million years ago. Dinohippus (center), a descendant of Eohippus, first appeared about 15 million years ago. Early Equus (right) evolved from Dinohippus.

Gradually, one-toed horse types developed from among the grazing types. They had larger bodies, longer legs, and enlarged jaws and skulls, and were thus much better adapted to grazing and running. Like *Hyracotherium*, the one-toed horse types seem to have originated in North and Central America, with one group known to have migrated to South America. Horse types also migrated across the still-existing Bering land bridge between Alaska and what is now Russia, but once this sank below the sea, European, African and Asian horse types were cut off from those in the Americas.

The one-toed horse type is known as *Equus*, and is the forerunner of the modern horse and its relatives such as the donkey and the zebra.

There were many different species of *Equus*, but most had become extinct by the end of the last Ice Age, including all those in North America. The types that survived in Europe and Asia diversified into larger and smaller types.

Right: This family tree shows how, over the course of about 55 million years a diversity of horse-like animals evolved from the four-toed Hyracotherium *(*Eohippus*). Many branches of the horse family died out, leaving one main group of one-toed horses from which* Equus, *the modern horse evolved.*

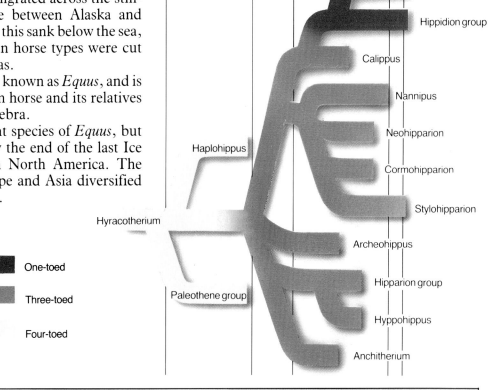

One-toed

Three-toed

Four-toed

Above: The zebra is one of the horse's closest relatives, also being descended from Equus. *It displays many features of primitive pony types, such as the upright mane and stocky body. Zebra markings sometimes appear on the flanks and legs of ancient breeds such as the Tarpan and the Mongolian Wild Horse.*

How Horses Spread

INFORMATION ON THE EARLY HORSE types is very incomplete, but it seems that they first spread from their evolutionary homeland in North America over land masses very different from today's continents. As the land masses split up at the end of the last Ice Age, horse groups developed simultaneously in different areas. However, because Australia split from the main land mass many millions of years before horse types migrated that far, no horses existed there until they were introduced by the early settlers during the 18th century. No early horse fossils have been found in Australia.

It is now thought that there were a number of different types of *Equus* in Europe and Asia, some being pony types, others more like small horses, and that they developed according to the environment in which they lived – those living in wild, wet areas remaining small, others in areas with good grazing growing larger.

It is also thought that these types became quite widely dispersed, and cross-bred, even before man intervened in the development of the horse.

Ever since man first domesticated the horse, in the Middle and Far East around 3000 BC, he has been instrumental in distributing the different horse types around the world.

The nomadic tribes of central Asia, who were probably the first people to domesticate the horse, would have taken their horses with them as they wandered across quite large areas of the continent. Conquering tribes took horses with them to pull their chariots, and to use as pack animals.

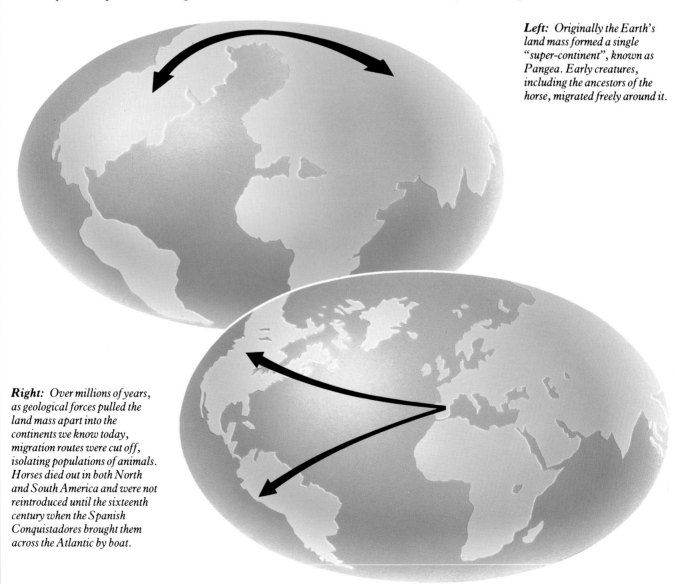

Left: Originally the Earth's land mass formed a single "super-continent", known as Pangea. Early creatures, including the ancestors of the horse, migrated freely around it.

Right: Over millions of years, as geological forces pulled the land mass apart into the continents we know today, migration routes were cut off, isolating populations of animals. Horses died out in both North and South America and were not reintroduced until the sixteenth century when the Spanish Conquistadores brought them across the Atlantic by boat.

When the Celts were driven into western Europe, and eventually to Britain, they took their Tarpan type horses (see page 132) and crossed them with indigenous horses to produce the Celtic pony, which they used to pull their chariots. In Britain, the Celtic pony provided the basis of many of the modern native breeds.

The Romans brought many different types of horses to Britain, including Friesian horses from northern Europe, from which the Dales and Fell ponies developed.

When the Moors invaded Europe, beginning in the 8th century, they brought with them many thousands of horses of Arab breeding, from which the Andalusian and many other European breeds were created.

In the 16th century the Spanish Conquistadores invaded America, taking with them a variety of ornately caparisoned Iberian, thereby re-introducing the horse into North America.

The horse had returned home.

Above: The Mongolian Pony is descended from the ancient native ponies of Mongolia, which the local tribes used as pack animals. These nomadic people traveled widely.

Below: At the Lascaux caves in southern France there are drawings of prehistoric horses that appear to resemble both the Mongolian Wild Horse of northeast Asia and the Exmoor Pony.

WHO DOMESTICATED THE HORSE

THE HORSE WAS DOMESTICATED in the Far East by early civilizations about 5,000 years ago (around 3,000 BC). Some experts believe this took place in Asiatic Russia and others in the ancient Fertile Crescent comprising Assyria and Babylonia. However, Stone Age drawings on rocks and in caves have shown what appears to be a head-collar of some kind, so it is possible that more primitive peoples had some kind of control or influence over early horses.

Initially, primitive tribes would have followed herds of wild horses, hunting them for meat. Domestication probably first occurred when young animals were captured and kept tethered or in pens. These animals were used for meat and milk, and would gradually have become accustomed to human attention. Mares in season would have been tethered on the outskirts of a tribe's territory, so that wild stallions could come and mate them.

These nomadic horse-owners soon realized that a horse could be made to carry goods and equipment, and so the horse began to be used as a pack animal. It has been suggested by historian Anthony Dent that the first riders were the pregnant wives of tribal leaders, who were put on horses to enable them to keep up with the tribe's nomadic wanderings.

The earliest widespread use of domesticated horses was as pack and harness animals. It is likely that even at this early stage in the history of the horse's domestication, the horse types diverged into harness types and riding types in different parts of the world, and that people traded in these different

Man began to ride horses quite early on, but in war early civilizations such as the Egyptians and Greeks used horses mainly to pull their chariots. The Persians, however, were excellent horsemen, and by 500 BC, had a powerful cavalry with horses able to carry heavy armor and weapons. The ancient Greeks were good horsemen, but the Romans, who had mounted cavalry were not especially so.

Below: A piece from the west side of the Parthenon Frieze (477-432 BC), showing two horsemen at canter taking part in a procession. Although bridles and bits had been invented at this stage, saddles had not. The Greeks were good horsemen, and took great interest in the best methods of training and riding horses.

Left: A Greek seal inscribed with the name of Darius I, who reigned from 548 to 486 BC. It depicts a king hunting from a horse-drawn chariot. Horses were used for drawing chariots long before they were ridden.

Below: An ancient Persian relief showing a battle between two mounted warriors. The ancient Persians were the first to use the horse for riding. They were excellent horsemen, and developed a very efficient cavalry.

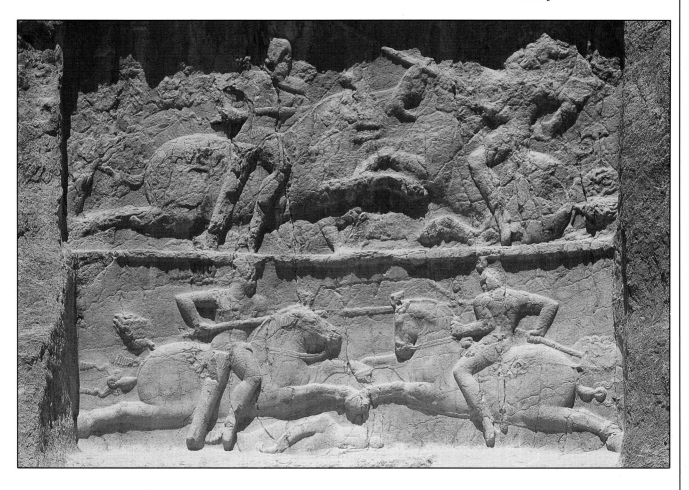

13

THE WORKING HORSE

SINCE IT WAS FIRST DOMESTICATED, the horse has been used for all types of work. Even today, every horse is, in practice, working for its living, whether it is a child's pony, a racehorse, or a farm horse.

In the beginning, the horse's main role was as a pack animal, and it continued to be used in this role up until the early part of the 20th century. To start with, the smaller, lighter types were used for this kind of work while the larger, more powerful animals were used as war horses. However, with the invention of fire-arms, armor was abandoned and a different type of horse was needed in battle, freeing the heavier horses for other types of work.

With the advent of industrialization heavy loads of equipment and goods needed to be moved across the country, and the very large, heavy draft breeds such as the Shire and the Clydesdale were developed. During the 19th century, horses were also used for towing barges along canals, and for moving coal and equipment around the coal-mines.

Horses have also played an important part in agriculture. In the beginning, plows were pulled by oxen, being too heavy for the lighter breeds of working horses. However, by the 18th century mechanized farm equipment was beginning to be used, speed and intelligence were needed in the animals being used to pull it, and draft horses came into their own for agricultural work.

Horses were also the main means of transport for people. As better roads began to be built in the 19th century, and the art of carriage-making reached its highest standards, coaches became lighter and faster, and very elegant horses, such as Trotters and Hackneys, were in demand to pull them.

With the arrival first of the railways and then the motor car, the horse was no longer needed for transport or agricultural work and it looked as if many of the draft breeds might die out. However, businesses are now realizing that, for short trips, horses are more economical for deliveries than motorized vans, and are beginning to use them.

Above: Horse-drawn buses were once a common sight. Animals used for public transportation, unlike the carriage-horses of the wealthy, often led a hard life, working on slippery cobbled streets.

Right: Heavy draft breeds like the Shire are often associated with agricultural work such as plowing. However, the very large draft breeds did not come into their own for this type of work until the end of the 18th century, when the invention of more sophisticated farm machinery required the use of horses that combined great physical strength with intelligence.

THE POLICE HORSE

It is in police work – for example, in the Royal Canadian Mounted Police (above) – that the horse/man relationship reaches one of its most refined levels. Police horses are trained to overcome almost completely their natural flight-or-fight instinct, and to face up to situations like violent crowds, gunfire and physical force from rioters. They must go wherever their rider asks, at any hour of the day or night, alone or in company, without question.

In their initial training, they are taught to approach a potentially frightening object or situation and are turned away from it, with great praise, just *before* the trainer feels the horse might object. In this way, the horse never develops resistance to its work, and comes to trust its rider implicitly.

Below: Although horses are no longer needed in most countries for farming and transportation several of the draft breeds from the heyday of the working horse, such as these Percherons, have survived, and are valued for their own sakes. They are used for demonstrations and showing, and in a small way for work.

Right: Ranching in Texas, where the horse is still used in one of its traditional working roles, for herding cattle. The Quarter-Horse, first bred in the eastern United States, was found to have a particular talent for this type of work. It was bred in large numbers and became the favorite horse of the cowboy.

THE HORSE IN WAR

IT IS TRULY SAID that empires have been built on the horse's back. Without the strength, speed and willingness of the horse to do man's bidding, all-conquering civilizations from the earliest days of the horse's domestication right up to the 20th century could not have conquered other peoples and spread their cultures throughout the world.

In the early days horses were used in battle mainly to pull chariots, but gradually the use of cavalry developed. The Persians, who were expanding their empire around 500 BC, used cavalry to great effect.

Much of the success of the Islamic empire as it

Above: *A section of the Bayeux Tapestry showing the Norman cavalry in action at the Battle of Hastings in 1066. By this time* *the Normans had developed a highly skilled cavalry, and the English foot-soldiers were no match for it.*

spread across most of Europe was due to its fast and highly disciplined cavalry. The European war-horse of this time, in contrast, was heavy and slow, as it had to carry up to 500 lb (225 kg) of arms and protective armor, as well as its rider, into battle.

With the invention of firearms, heavy armor became obsolete, and new types of cavalry developed. These fell into three groups. The dragoons were mounted on heavy, cob types; the lancers were mounted on lighter horses, and were used for sudden assaults and fast flanking movements; and the Hussars, also used for sudden attacks, were also mounted on light, fast horses.

During the 19th century, with the development of shrapnel and automatic weapons, the value of the cavalry charge gradually declined, although horses were still used for artillery and troop movements, and very large numbers of horses were used in all campaigns until after World War I.

In World War I, well-loved family horses, chil-

HORSE ARMOR

In the Middle Ages, armor reached its zenith as horse and rider were clad in more and more concealing plates of intricately jointed metal, which, of course, became increasingly heavy. Knights often had to be hoisted onto their horses.

Horses' face-plates often had spikes on the forehead, giving the horse the appearance of a metal unicorn. The body armor covered the whole horse down to its elbows and stifles, protruding at the front to allow for foreleg and knee movement. Neck armour was also made from jointed plates of metal to allow for movement.

Horse armor continued to be used until the end of the 16th-century by which time the increasing use of firearms and cannon had rendered it obsolete. The illustration shows early 16th-century Spanish armor.

dren's ponies and commercial horses were commandeered into the army by force, never to be returned to their families or owners. To put down a horse rather than allow it to be taken was regarded as treason. In modern times horses are used by armies all over the world for ceremonial purposes.

Above: *The Charge of the Light Brigade in 1854 was one of the most disastrous cavalry charges ever. Out of 673 horses that charged the Russian artillery, only 260 survived. The development of automatic weapons and shrapnel during the 19th century gradually made massed cavalry charges of this sort obsolete.*

Left: *During World War I millions of horses were used on all parts of the front, and losses were appalling. The Scots Greys arrived at the Belgian frontier soon after the outbreak of war, and the famous gray horses had to be stained chestnut in order to camouflage them and prevent the enemy identifying their formation.*

17

THE SPORTING HORSE

Left: The Master and Huntsman of a French hunt. Hunting is one of the oldest sports. In the past many different animals were hunted, but for the last two centuries, the fox has been the most popular quarry in most countries.

Below: Polo is one of the roughest, toughest games played today, and playing in the snow adds an extra dimension of excitement. Polo ponies must be brave and obedient; they must be able to stop and turn like lightning.

EQUESTRIAN SPORTS go from strength to strength, and are increasingly popular with both riders and spectators. One of the oldest surviving horseback sports is hunting. In the beginning, the stag was the main quarry, but now, in English-speaking countries, it is the fox. In both the USA and Australia, hunting is based on the British model.

Polo is another ancient sport, and is thought to have originated in Persia about 2000 years ago. From there it spread to China, Mongolia, Japan, and eventually India, where it was discovered by the British in the 19th century. Its popularity has since spread all over the world. It makes exacting demands on the horses, requiring considerable speed, agility, stamina and courage.

Horse-racing has been popular around the world for many centuries, but since the early 18th century it has developed into a major sporting industry.

Another sport that is increasing in popularity is driving, and many breeds of horse that were originally used as carriage-horses have found a new role in this sport. Combined driving, which was introduced in 1969, is the equivalent of a three-day event, and includes a dressage test, a cross-country marathon, and an obstacle-course in the show-ring.

Horse shows that included both competitive events and showing classes began to be held in the late 19th century. These came to include show-jumping and dressage events as well as the show classes in which horses are judged on type and conformation (make and shape). The latter are more leisurely but can be just as exciting to their enthusiasts, and even tiny children can compete in

Above: The ancient Chinese, Tartars, Mongols and Greeks all raced their horses. In modern times, racing as a sport took off with the development of the Thoroughbred, which is still the fastest breed of horse in the world.

lead-line classes, which sets many off on the road to becoming a champion.

The breeding of horses for competition rather than military use has resulted in finer, faster horses, even in carriage-driving, and has improved many breeds, or at least changed them beyond all recognition. This particularly applies to the many European warm-blood breeds such as the Hanoverian, the Holstein and the Trakehner, which now have a great deal of Thoroughbred blood in them to provide the speed, quality and quick reactions needed in today's sports horse.

Many forms of equine competition involve large sums of money, both paid for and won by horses, as well as sponsorship deals, but the main attraction for the public lies in watching the superb achievements and performances of racehorses, show-jumpers, eventers, carriage-horses, trotters and pacers.

THE OLYMPIC SPORTS

The three modern Olympic equestrian sports are show-jumping, dressage and eventing.

Show-jumping
The origins of show-jumping lie in hunting. At the Dublin Show in 1868, a "high leap" and a "wide leap" were first used to test horses for the hunting field. In 1881 a permanent jumping course was built there and show-jumping began to develop as a sport in its own right. In France in 1900, jumping competitions were held with the Olympic Games.

Dressage
Dressage developed from the high-school equitation of the 15th to 18th centuries which was popular in the royal courts of Europe. Movements that had originally been developed for use in battle were combined into a demonstration of horsemanship that showed off the stamina, agility and obedience of the horse and the skills of the rider.

Eventing
The origins of eventing lie in the battlefield, as it developed out of the endurance rides that were used to test cavalry horses. At the beginning of the 20th century, the first three-day event was held, in France. It began with a dressage test, followed by a gruelling cross-country endurance ride, and concluded with a show-jumping test (added partly to increase public interest in eventing). At this time three-day events were purely military affairs, and it was not until after World War II that civilians could compete. Eventing was first included in the Olympics in 1912, and is the ultimate all-round test of a horse.

Show-jumping

Dressage

Eventing

DO HORSES THINK?

HORSES CERTAINLY DO THINK – to survive in the wild over millions of years they have had to develop the ability to think extremely quickly (although their initial "startle" reflex on becoming aware of dangers such as a predator is more instinct than thinking). Once they have become aware of a potential danger, they must quickly assess the situation, and decide whether or not to run away, or just move to keep the danger outside their personal space.

Some horses seem to show more intelligent thought than others. For example, some work out quite quickly how to undo their stable bolts and escape – a few even learn how to undo the doors of other horses in the barn and let out the occupants. This requires both planning and understanding of the outcome of their action.

The ability to look ahead shows high-level thinking ability, and although horses may not be able to plan and look ahead to the extent that humans can, they understand time and know that certain things will happen at a certain time of day, for example feed times. If a horse is thirsty, it has to think to go to the water source. If it is in a field at feed time, it shows thinking ability by wandering over to the gate and looking expectantly (looking ahead) in the direction from which you will come with its feed bucket.

In order, for example, to complete a round of jumps, the horse has to concentrate quite hard, thinking about the various aids its rider is giving it and what they mean – more impulsion, slow down, turn here – and it has to realize that the jump its rider has aimed it at is the one it is required to clear. It then has to gauge its own strides, or perhaps regulate them in accordance with its rider's instructions, and take off into the air in the right place. Only the horse itself can decide, by thinking quickly, just how high to propel itself into the air. This takes considerable judgement, even with experience and practice, and cannot be done without clear thought.

REASONING POWER

It is often said that horses have no reasoning power, reasoning being the ability to think out a problem or situation and overcome it. Many experienced and sensitive horsepeople deny this, knowing from their own experience that horses *can* solve problems. In one informal experiment, horses were given feeds in buckets with loose lids which they had to remove before they could eat. Most of the horses clearly considered the situation and by various means removed the lids calmly. Only a few bashed frustratedly at the buckets, showing no ability to think through the problem.

In another incident, a mare was caught by one hind leg in a loose wire fence. She was seen to turn her head and look for several seconds at the loop of wire round her leg. She then raised her other hind leg, felt the wire carefully with her (shod) hoof, stepped on the loop pressing it down to the ground, and freed her trapped leg. This is an obvious example of clear thought and reasoning power.

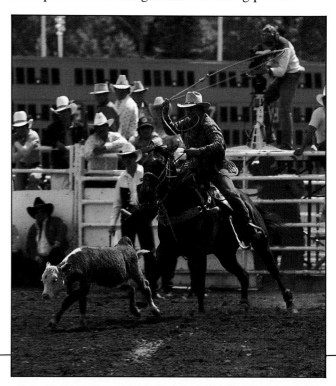

Above: *Mares and foals in domesticity are usually weaned earlier than would happen in the wild. If they are reunited, they will recognize each other.*

Right: *Horses that work with cattle have to be very quick thinking to anticipate the direction the steer or calf will take, and to react instantly.*

REACTING TO A THREAT

A horse confronted by something frightening or potentially dangerous will analyse the threat and respond according to the perceived seriousness of the danger. Initially it will show the "startle response" – it will raise its head, prick up its ears and point them forward, flare its nostrils to take in potentially informative smells and open its eyes wide to see as much as possible. Its body will be tense and its hind legs will come slightly more forward under the body ready to take its weight if the danger is such that it decides to wheel round and gallop off to safety.

If in the case, for example, of an intruder, the horse decides to stand its ground, it will probably thrust its head forward aggressively, with ears back, nostrils wrinkled up and back and maybe bare its teeth and open the mouth as a warning of its intention to bite if the threatening intruder does not retreat. Should the intruder *not* retreat, it will threaten more aggressively, moving forward with the expression described, maybe with head low and neck stretched out, lunging out at the intruder with its teeth.

If, in the case of a horse intruder, the other horse does not withdraw, a fight may ensue. Both horses will maintain an angry, aggressive expression and they will bite at eaoh other anywhere within reach. Males, in particular, often rear up with flailing forelegs, trying to come down on to the back of their opponent and get them down onto the ground where they can be trampled and kicked. They also back into each other, kicking out rapidly in succession with both hind feet at once. Such kicking is a more common method of fighting for mares.

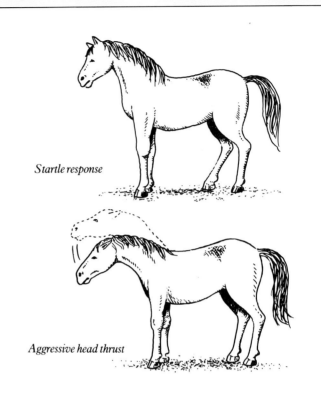

Startle response

Aggressive head thrust

Moving to attack

Fighting

HOW HORSES LEARN

SURVIVAL IN THE WILD is often dependent on an ability to adapt rapidly to new conditions. Horses can learn fast if the right training is given.

Horses learn mainly by means of association of ideas. It has been scientifically and practically proved that if a horse can be made to associate a particular task, even an unpleasant or frightening one, with something pleasant he will tolerate it much more readily. For instance, a horse that does not like being shod will accept it in time if it learns that it will be fed some favourite titbits, or have a net of sweet hay to nibble at, during the process. If you are trying to teach a horse to move over in the stable, for example by pushing it so that it moves away, and at the same time saying "over", it soon learns to associate the push with the action and before long will move over to a slight pressure on its side or just the word "over". The position of the handler's body is important too. For example, if you stand directly in front of or behind it when saying "over", it will not know which way to move.

Horses learn their daily routine quickly and watch the goings on, listen to the various sounds, and absorb daily happenings. They quickly associate the rattle of feed buckets with the appearance of feed, for instance, and the sight of someone carrying their saddle and bridle with work or going for a hack.

They are also quick to absorb atmosphere and can differentiate between a pleased, praising or calming tone in the human voice and a sharp, cross, reprimanding tone, or an urging, encouraging one.

Below: *At the beginning of its training, the horse learns basic commands like "walk on" and "whoa" on the lunge. Being led by a helper, the horse is shown* *what the different sounds mean. Soon it learns the commands well enough to work mainly from the voice alone.*

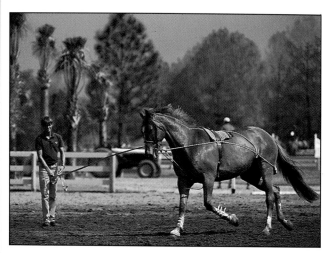

KEEP IT SIMPLE

Horses learn short, simple sounds best. Although a stream of words said in a particular tone can convey your feelings – such as calming down or urging on – when you want the horse to perform a particular movement it is best to use short sounds of up to three

Below: *Racehorses are introduced to starting stalls as youngsters by being walked through them, then standing in* *them; they soon learn that the gates flying open means "gallop".*

CIRCUS HORSE

Circus horses, particularly those touring the same route every year, often have to learn new acts regularly, as their audiences will want to see something different each time. However, they never forget their old routines, and can usually be put through a movement after several years' break and perform it faultlessly. Even just the sound of a particular tune can set them off on an old routine.

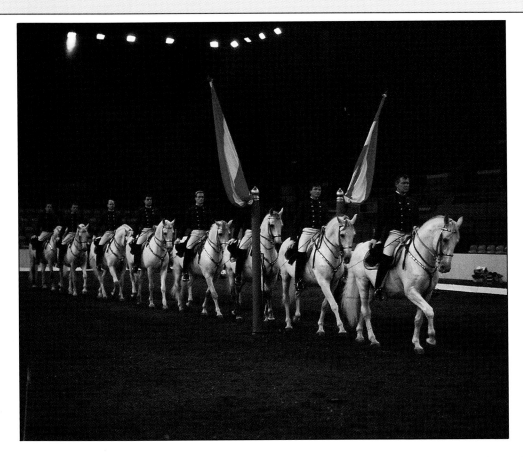

Left: To reach the high standards required at the Spanish Riding School, horses must learn movements that are progressively more difficult, both mentally and physically; they must show increasing understanding of their riders' requirements, and respond to finer and finer aids.

syllables. As horses recognize the actual sound, the tone and inflection of the voice is very important. Always give commands in the same way so as not to confuse the horse. When you buy a new horse, ask the previous owner to demonstrate the exact way in which he or she gave it commands so you can imitate them, even down to their accent if necessary. If the previous owner asked the horse to "trot on" and you use the long drawn-out command "terr-ot", you cannot blame the horse for not complying.

REWARD VERSUS PUNISHMENT

Horses are easily upset and startled, so it is best to use reward training rather than punishment training. For instance, when a horse does something right praise it consistently by always using the words "good boy" said in the same tone. If it does something wrong, however, it's best to give no response at all but make your aids clearer, then praise it when it does get it right. Most horses do want to please.

There are times when a horse may be blatantly naughty or dominating. In such cases, *one* sharp smack or crack of the whip used *at the same time* as saying the word "no" crossly, delivered the instant it does wrong, will convey the message that this behavior is not wanted.

It is essential that both praise and punishment are administered within one second of the horse's action, otherwise the horse cannot connect your response with whatever it did and will learn nothing. It must associate your action with its own, good or bad, in order to learn whether you are pleased or not. This is the way its brain works and is essential to the learning process.

INADVERTENT LEARNING

If a horse comes to associate an action with something unpleasant it will not want to do it. For example, if a horse receives a painful jab in the mouth every time it jumps, it will quickly learn that jumping means pain and will start refusing; if it is kicked on the hip every time it is mounted it will soon start to become difficult to mount, having learned that the process is unpleasant.

HOW HORSES SLEEP

HORSES NEED SLEEP just as much as humans do, but they don't need the same amount. They need about 4 hours sleep out of every 24, and take it in roughly half-hour snatches rather than all in one go. The reason for this is, again, their prey/predator lifestyle, which so frequently spills over into domesticity. As creatures of wide open spaces, often with little natural protection such as a lair or den, the horse needs to be constantly on the alert for danger. If it were to spend several hours at a stretch deeply asleep, it would be easy prey for a hunting animal, so it has evolved to sleep for short periods.

The horse does not always sleep at night, but takes some of its sleep during daylight, if allowed to. Many horses that have had morning exercise like to lie down for a nap after their midday feed, imitating the sleep pattern they would adopt in the wild. This can also be seen in horses turned out in fields, who often lie down during the day.

Apart from dozing, there are two kinds of sleep, SWS (short wave sleep) and REM (rapid eye movement) sleep. Experiments using electrodes to detect electrical brain waves have shown that in shallow sleep the brain waves are of a short frequency (SWS): the brain is quite inactive but the sleep is fairly shallow and the horse can be easily awakened.

Deep sleep is experienced when the brain waves are longer. The brain is active during this type of sleep, but the body goes almost into a torpor, making the horse easy to approach but difficult to wake up. During this sleep, the eyes move rapidly from side to side beneath the eyelids, which is why it is called rapid eye movement (REM) sleep. Because the body seems to lose muscle tone during REM sleep, the horse has to lie completely relaxed and flat out on its side in order to experience it, whereas in SWS it can sleep propped on its breastbone. It is likely that horses, like humans, dream during REM sleep.

Lying flat out is obviously dangerous in the wild as it takes a horse several vital seconds to get to its feet and gallop off. It is much safer for the horse to lie propped up as it can get up much more quickly.

From a management point of view, it is essential to give a horse a large enough stall to allow it to lie flat out and experience the deep, refreshing and essential REM sleep, and to give it a dry, clean, soft bed so it won't be reluctant to lie down and rest. The horse must have enough room that it does not become cast, which happens when it rolls over and becomes trapped on its back because its legs strike the wall of the stall. Horses always pick a smooth, *dry* spot to

Below: *In this position a horse will doze, and can also experience short-wave sleep (SWS), a shallow kind of sleep.*

To be able to sleep standing up was a great advantage to the horse in the wild, because it could be off at a gallop within seconds.

Left: *Horses have a special arrangement of "locking" joints and ligaments in their elbows and stifles. When the horse sleeps standing up, these joints lock, propping up the horse on its forehand. It can even relax one hind leg and still not fall over.*

sleep when they have a choice: those kept on wet land in winter may be reluctant to lie down often enough, particularly flat out, and may deprive themselves of sleep as a result. Such horses should have access to a well bedded down, roomy run-in barn or large shelter.

CAN HORSES SLEEP STANDING UP?

Yes, they can and do. Again, this is a safety feature from the wild. If they are already on their feet (in which position they can either doze or experience SWS) they can be off at a gallop within a couple of seconds of being alerted, usually by other horses or by a sound.

There is a special arrangement of "locking" joints and ligaments in their elbows and stifles (another safety feature) which props the horse on its forelegs keeping it upright. It can rest one hind leg (joints bent, hip down) during this process and still not fall over, but not a foreleg. When alerted, up comes its head throwing the weight on to its hindquarters, which gather underneath it ready to propel it forward out of danger.

Left: *Horses need to lie flat out in order to experience REM (rapid eye movement) or deep sleep. Horses whose stalls are too small, or who feel that they don't have room to lie out like this may deprive themselves of this type of sleep, and become over-tired, short-tempered or even neurotic as a result.*

HOW HORSES SEE

THE HORSE'S EYES are ideal for its existence as a plainsdwelling, grass-eating prey animal, and are similar to those of other prey animals, for example cattle and antelope. Such animals need the widest possible field of vision so that they can see potential predators approaching more or less from all directions. Their eyes are set on the sides of the head, rather than at the front like predators such as cats, dogs and humans. In their natural state grass-eaters spend a good 16 hours a day with their heads down, grazing. This position gives them the ability to see all around with a small turn of the head whilst still eating, without moving the body as humans need to do if they want to see clearly behind them. The only obstruction to the horse's vision in this position is its four thin legs, so it is ideally equipped for most of the time to spot danger. This is the main reason for its good survival rate in the wild, and explains why it is not easy to approach horses in a field without being noticed.

The accompanying diagram shows the horse's actual field of vision when it is looking straight ahead. Its vision is mainly "monocular" (single-eyed), that is, it mostly sees its surroundings as two pictures, one from each eye. This indicates that it is probably capable of thinking about two things at

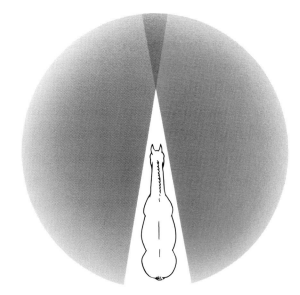

Above: *The horse's eyes are set on the sides of its head, and it sees two different pictures, one with each eye. This gives it a very wide field of vision. The small* *V-shaped area directly in front of its head is the only area where it can see with both eyes and therefore clearly judge distances.*

once, at the same time as grazing. It has "binocular" (two-eyed) vision directly in front of it for judging clearly how far away an object is, and to enable it to assess accurately the route in front of it when moving.

For many years the horse was described as having a "ramped retina," because its retina (the screen at the back of the eye on which rays of light carrying images focused) was thought to be sloped. This would require the horse to move its head to bring the images into focus. It is now known that the central part of the retina gives the clearest picture, and this is the reason for the horse's various head movements when trying to see something. It moves its head to direct the rays through the eye lens (which is not so flexible as in human beings) to direct them on to the center of the retina.

The most significant point to emerge is that in order for the horse to have clear vision and, therefore, peace of mind and security, it must have reasonable freedom to move its head and neck as it wishes. If the rider restricts its head unduly, by means of either reins, or equipment such as martingales which "strap down" the head, they are partially blinding the horse. This is one reason why a horse not only goes unwillingly, but may fight for its head. The other reason is that a horse naturally panics if over-restricted. Freedom of its head and neck is particularly important when a horse is

Below: *The horse's field of vision enables it to see almost all around it. This gives it the advantage that while it is grazing, it only has to turn its* *head slightly in order to check that there is no danger approaching from any direction. It is almost impossible to approach unnoticed.*

Left: *The harness of draught horses usually incorporates blinkers to prevent the horse from becoming alarmed by the traffic and other distracting sights that usually surround it in a busy street. The blinkers of these Shire horses belonging to a British brewery keep their attention focused on the road ahead.*

moving fast or jumping, as it *must* have clear vision to judge the ground, and the size of obstacles.

To see clearly close in front of it, the horse must arch its neck and draw in its muzzle into a "collected" position. This directs the rays of light through the top part of the pupil on to the center of the retina. If you watch your horse, you'll see it do this to look at you or something you are carrying when close to it, or to inspect some close-up object or the ground in front of it.

GLORIOUS TECHNICOLOR

Horse spectrum

Human spectrum

An old belief of some horsemen was that horses are color blind. Research shows, however, that they do have similar color-discerning cells in their eyes to those in humans. They can, it seems, see yellow best, and orange and red. They can distinguish green quite well but have difficulty with blue and violet. It is important to school your horse over different colored jumps and use all the colors of the spectrum to accustom it to anything it might meet in the jumping arena.

The horse's pupil is a horizontal oval rather than a circle, giving it a wide but rather shallow panoramic field of vision, and it can be easily startled by things not quite in view above its head. Young horses backed for the first time are often frightened by a rider sitting up above them. It's advisable for the rider to crouch low over the withers at first, gradually assuming a more upright position.

The inability to perceive depth, except when looking immediately in front of it, accounts for the fact that the horse will shy sideways away from something which startles it because it cannot tell what it is. It will, if permitted, turn and face the object head on, from a safe distance, look at it with both eyes and satisfy its curiosity.

IT'S KEEPING ITS EYE ON YOU

When you are riding, your horse can see your legs, whether or not you are carrying a whip, and when you move it to use it (which is why it may often anticipate your whip aid and move before you apply it). When you are riding a bend or a circle, its inside eye can make visual contact with yours, if you position the horse correctly, and you can just about look each other in the eye.

HOW HORSES HEAR

HORSES ARE VERY SENSITIVE to sound, and can hear high- and low-pitched noises that humans are unable to pick up.

The *pinna*, or funnel part of the ear, picks up the sound waves and directs them down inside the head where a network of bones and chambers together with the eardrum transmit and amplify them for special nerves to pick up. These nerves in turn transmit these messages to the brain, which translates the sounds into meaning if they are familiar, or alerts the horse to something strange in its environment if they are not.

A horse does not automatically panic at an unfamiliar sound; it will pay attention to it and remember it. If something happens at the same time as the sound, it will, in future, associate the happening with that sound, and this is an important part of training and learning.

Horses' hearing is sharper than that of humans; they can hear things like other horses calling, car engines (which they can tell from each other) and doors opening, before a person can pick them up and from much further away. Horses that are boarded out, for example, soon come to recognize their owners' car engines and associate the noise with the appearance of that particular person. They will often pick up the sound long before the staff in the stable.

Horses are extremely sensitive to the nature of a sound and its volume. There is never any need to shout at a horse unless it is a very dominant animal either attacking or really pushing its weight around, in which case volume can help get the better of it. *Tone* of voice is usually more effective than volume; a cross growl when the horse is doing wrong, and an up-and-down, pleased tone for praise.

Screaming and screeching often frighten horses, whereas soft monotones calm them down. However, some sounds which might be thought to frighten them, such as blasting in a quarry or police sirens, do not always do so.

Horses are as agitated by constant, raucous sound as humans are. In racing stables, for instance, the best trainers insist on a quiet period during the afternoon after morning work, grooming and the midday feed, so that the horses can lie down and rest or have a sleep.

Some horses prefer a busy atmosphere where they can see and hear what is going on around them, and others like peace and quiet. It is important to watch your horse and try to tell by its behavior and expression which category it falls into. If it seems slightly (or very) tense, its ears flicking around a lot, not resting much during the day, it could be that there is too much noise going on for its liking.

MUSIC

Experiments carried out with mares at the Irish National Stud some years ago showed that horses like music, but are selective in their tastes. Most

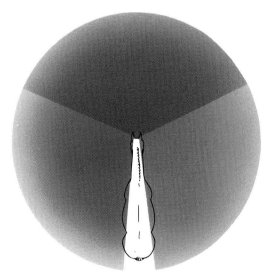

Above: *The position of the horse's ears on the sides of its head enables it to hear almost all around it. Each ear can pick up sounds to the front and side, leaving a gap immediately behind it which it can cover with a small turn of its head.*

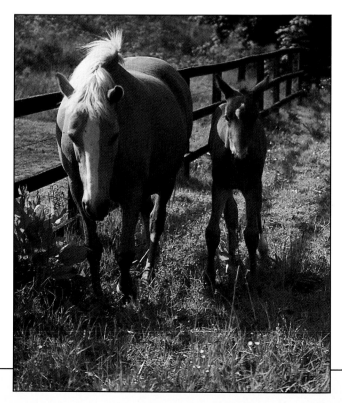

horses like calming or cheerful instrumental music and are agitated by heavy, loud unmelodious music such as rock. Vocal music is also not as welcome to them as instrumental music.

Dressage performed to music is now popular in many countries and the horses really seem to enjoy it. They appear perky, majestic, calm or energetic according to the music chosen for their routine. Like circus horses, they often associate the music with particular movements.

Remember that your horse is a prisoner in its stall. You may enjoy having a radio playing while you work, but see whether your horse enjoys it as much as you do. Never leave a radio on all the time as it can really get on a horse's nerves, and be selective about the programs you tune in to, and the type of music played. The horse has to rely on you for both its entertainment and its peace and quiet.

LOVE CALLING!

Another experiment done at the Irish National Stud was that of playing the sound of a stallion calling to an in-season mare to study the effect this had on the brood mares stabled in a particular barn. It was found that those in season and ready to mate showed signs of being amenable to the stallion even though he was not present, and those not in season came into season after a very few days of the sound being played to them intermittently.

Left: The mare has one ear back and one forward, indicating that she is listening to what is going on all around.

Above: The horse on the right is interested in what is going on around it, while its companion is showing signs of annoyance.

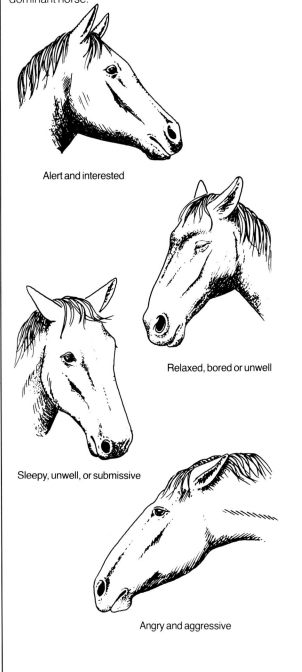

THE LANGUAGE OF EARS

The position of the ears is one of the most important indicators of a horse's mood and intentions. Ears pricked forward are a sign of alert curiosity and good mood. Ears turned back are often a sign of relaxation, or even boredom. They may also be a sign that the horse is unwell. The ears pressed flat against the head are a classic sign of bad temper and aggression. It can also signify that the horse is feeling stressed. When the ears flop to either side, it may be a sign of sleepiness or sickness. It is also a typical sign of submission to a more dominant horse.

Alert and interested

Relaxed, bored or unwell

Sleepy, unwell, or submissive

Angry and aggressive

HOW HORSES COMMUNICATE

ALTHOUGH THEY DON'T HAVE A LANGUAGE, horses express themselves very clearly to other horses, and to humans who can understand their various facial expressions and general body language. Horses have, in addition, a very wide range of vocal sounds for expressing feelings, and possibly giving commands. Smell is also important among horses in understanding the status and condition of another horse, and sometimes of humans too.

Dominant or happy horses communicate this by making themselves look as big and impressive as possible. The head is up, the ears usually up and forward, the gait is prancing and the tail is out and up. Submissive or unhappy (or sick) horses actually *look* smaller. The head is often down, the ears flopping sideways or held softly backwards, it is listless or moves with no great energy or panache, and the tail is held low or even pressed down between the buttocks in fear.

It is important to be able to recognize the signs of anger in a horse, because an angry horse threatening to bite or kick can do serious injury. Its ears will be back, and it will have an angry expression in its eyes. The skin will appear to be drawn tightly on its face, the nostrils will be wrinkled up and back and the

mouth may be open if it is thinking of biting. The tail may thrash about quite strongly (this alone is often seen in horses with a very dominant rider, particularly if they themselves are dominant horses who don't like being told what to do). If the horse is going to kick, or warning that it may, a hind leg will be raised and the hoof waved about or carefully aimed.

If the horse you are riding behaves like this, it could simply be annoyed at being ridden, or at the general situation, or angry with a nearby horse

Above: Your relationship with your horse is as individual as that with your friends. It is impossible to say why two people, two horses, or a horse and a person hit it off and become friends; there is an intangible "chemistry" between the two.

Left: Horses are gregarious, social animals who live naturally in herds, associating closely with other herd members. Even in herds, however, they like to maintain a certain "personal space"; only foals with dams and close friends are regularly allowed to invade another's space.

MEETING A NEW HORSE

It is said that the first 30 seconds are vital when meeting someone new, and when meeting a horse for the first time the same holds true. The wrong way to do it is to go straight up to the horse, pat it on the head and start ordering it around, tacking it up, or whatever. This is completely against the method horses use with each other, and you will succeed only in alienating it.

Speak the horse's name as you approach it slightly from one side. Stand a few paces away to let it look at you; then approach it calmly, with your arms down, and go close enough to let it smell you, as it would another horse. Let it take several seconds, then quietly raise your hand and *stroke* (not pat) the bottom of its neck, gradually working your way to its withers. Scratch it gently, talking quietly all the time and watching its reaction to you. Then, if you have a treat for it, give it your offering on the flat of your hand – and you may well end up with a friend for life.

(maybe an enemy), or irritated by uncomfortable tack or bad riding. You must work out which, because the horse can only communicate its displeasure, not describe what is annoying it. If riding near an angry horse, move away from it. If you are on the ground and handling a horse displaying these signs, be extremely careful to keep hold of its head (if you suspect a bite) and to keep away from its back legs (if you expect a kick).

VOCAL CALLS

Horse sounds range from a soft whicker of affection from a mare to her foal, to a blood-curdling scream from one stallion to a rival.

A neigh is a fairly loud, high, vibrating noise used to call to horses in the distance or to find out, by listening for an answering neigh, if there are any other horses nearby. A whinny is a softer, lower neigh given to greet a friend, equine or human, and may become excited and stronger when the horse is expecting food, or a stallion approaches a mare.

Squeals, short and sharp, can mean the horse has experienced a sudden pain, or can be an expression of play-feeling. Horses suffering from colic or laminitis often groan and grunt pitifully.

SMELLS

These are not consciously given off, but the smells one horse gives out are statements to others, although humans do not have a sufficiently sensitive sense of smell to recognize them. Mares in season, in particular, give off very specific scents to stallions, who recognize just when they are ready for mating.

When people are afraid they give off a specific smell which horses, at least, recognize easily. A horse may react by dominating its handler if it feels superior, or by becoming nervous if it is submissive.

RELATIONSHIPS WITH HUMANS

Horses are gregarious, social, herd animals, and as in most societies, there are bosses, followers and in-betweeners in horse herds. The majority of horses are followers or in-betweeners and need human leadership from their trainers and handlers to feel settled and secure, and there is usually no need for very firm discipline with such animals. With dominant, natural leaders the situation can be different, requiring firm (but not violent or cruel) handling from a skilled handler or trainer. However, if a dominant horse can be made to respect its handler and form a partnership it will often try its heart out for its rider, and some of the best competitive horse-and-rider teams have comprised such horses. Dominant horses recognize dominant humans. They only browbeat weak or bullying ones: the first type they dominate, as in nature, and the second they may well fight, again as in nature.

In the human world it is safest for a human, who understands the environment and circumstances, to be "boss."

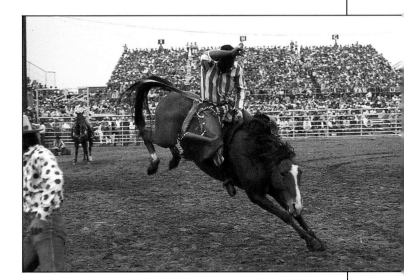

Above: *Rodeo horses like this bucking bronco are chosen for their propensity for bucking. A good deal of discomfort and mental distress are inflicted on these horses, and they cannot be blamed for hating the sight of humans.*

POINTS OF THE HORSE

CONFORMATION, or the make and shape of a horse, is a most important subject for anyone choosing a horse, especially if the horse has to compete or otherwise work hard.

UNDERSTANDING TERMS

A horse that is *short coupled* has a shortish back, and you cannot fit more than a hand's width between its last rib and the point of its hip. This makes for strength and handiness. *Slack loins* are the opposite of *short coupled*, indicating a rather long, weak back and possibly clumsy action.

Well let-down refers to the hocks, which should be "down near the ground": the lower part of the hind legs should be noticeably shorter than the upper part for more efficient leverage and less likelihood of tendon strain. The points of the hocks should be level with the front chestnuts when viewed from the sides. The front cannons should, similarly, be shorter than the forearm.

If a horse has a *deep girth*, it has plenty of depth and room for the heart and lungs. The length of the legs should not exceed the depth of the body from withers to breastbone.

Below: *Some of the horse's major organs. The horse's digestive system is specially adapted to deal with its natural diet of grass. The stomach is relatively small compared with that of a cow, and food is mainly broken down in the colon (large intestine) which is relatively large. Cellulose – the main component of grass – is broken down by the action of bacteria and digestive juices in this part of the digestive tract.*

Right: *One system for assessing the horse's conformation is to look at the relative lengths of sections of the body:*
$a=b=d=e$
$c=\frac{1}{2}a$
The distance from shoulder to knee should be more than from knee to ground. The distance from hock to stifle is more than from hock to ground. The hocks should be on a level with the front chestnuts. The angle of the shoulder should be 45° to the upright. The pastern/fetlock angle should be 45°.

If a horse has too-long legs, it is said to *show a lot of daylight* – in other words, a lot of space or daylight shows beneath its body. If it's short-legged and compact, it *doesn't show much daylight* – a good point.

Open elbows mean that you can fit your fist between the elbow and the ribcage, a very good point which should ensure a long reach (stride) with the forelegs so that the horse *covers a lot of ground* with each stride and therefore uses less energy.

Standing over a lot of ground means that the horse appears to stand squarely with *a leg at each corner*, rather than having its legs bunched together underneath it, which is a bad point.

A horse described as *croup high* has the point of its croup higher than its withers. This is quite a bad point as the saddle will for ever be sliding forwards and digging in behind the shoulders, which can make the horse very sore and injure muscles and skin. It also gives the rider an unpleasant "going downhill" feeling. The croup should be level with the withers or slightly lower for ordinary riding.

Length of rein refers to the distance between the horse's mouth and the rider's hand. A good length here provides the security of knowing that you have *plenty in front of you*, and are not likely to go over the

GETTING YOUR EYE IN

The best way to imprint on your mind a picture of a well-conformed horse is to visit top level shows and really study the top few horses in each class noting the general proportions of the different points or areas of the horse. This takes time and practice, but by looking at the best, and, after a few weeks, at those near the bottom of the line-up, you will be able to recognize good and bad conformation.

horse's head too easily should it stop suddenly. Good length of rein depends on the horse having correctly proportioned neck and shoulders. If it has, it is described as *having a good front*. If not, it has a *poor front* or is *short in front*.

The shoulder of a riding horse should be *well sloped*, the horse being described as having *sloping shoulders*. The angle from the point of the shoulder to the point of the wither, should be about 40° or 45°, and should be the same as the angle formed by the pasterns and feet with the ground. The hind feet and pastern angle (called the foot/pastern axis) can be *slightly* more upright. Pasterns that are too long and sloping can be weak, whereas upright pasterns make for an uncomfortable ride.

COLORS AND MARKINGS

COAT COLOR and markings developed over millions of years to give the animal the best possible camouflage for the area in which it lived. The more closely it resembled its background, the less likelihood there was of its being spotted by a predator.

One of the most primitive horse and pony colors is dun (a yellowy beige) with black points (the points being mane, forelock, tail and the lower legs). In a woodland background or plains environment where by no means everything is a lush green, duns are extremely well camouflaged.

Old stories abound of good and bad colors in horses. Chestnut horses were supposedly hot tempered, black nasty tempered and lacking in stamina, bay and brown dependable, and so on. The truth is that color has no bearing whatsoever on temperament or performance ability.

The only exceptions to this are horses who have pink skin under white hair (and some white-haired horses have dark skin underneath). These horses are much more susceptible to the weather than others, because pink skin lacks the strengthening substance melanin which is responsible for skin and hair color. The pink hue comes from blood circulating

Below: Within these color categories there are different shades and varieties. If there is any doubt about the color of a horse, it is decided by the color of the points – the muzzle, tips of the ears, mane and tail, and lower part of the legs.

Black

Dark bay

Light bay

Liver chestnut

Chestnut

Dun

Strawberry roan

Palomino

Piebald

Skewbald

Odd-colored

Blue roan

Dapple gray

Fleabitten gray

Gray

Albino

ANCESTRY

Asiatic Wild Stock

Arab

battle over the heavy war horses of the Europeans soon became apparent. Once the Moors had been driven out of Spain, the Arab horses that were left behind were crossed with native horses to produce a new type of battle horse, the Andalusian, that was still large and powerful, yet also fast and very agile. The Arab's reputation for stamina, speed and agility quickly spread, and it was soon in demand throughout Europe for cross-breeding with local horses.

The Arab's ability to stamp its conformation and soundness, its free, floating action, stamina and gentle nature on all its offspring have made it very popular for founding and refining other breeds, with the result that it has had more influence on the world's horse population than any other breed. All warm-blood breeds contain Arab blood, as do many pony breeds, and even a few of the cold-blood breeds.

The Arab is still as popular as ever and Arab breeding farms exist in countries all over the world. However, there is a danger that indiscriminate breeding in order to supply this demand could lead to a deterioration.

In addition to being popular for cross-breeding, the Arab makes a good riding horse. And although the pure-bred Arab is not used for show-jumping or eventing, it is ideally suited to competitive events like endurance riding.

Below: *An Arab foal with its mother. The Arab has the capacity to stamp its qualities on all its offspring, and is in as much demand as ever around the* *world for founding and improving other breeds. The purity of the breed is jealously guarded by Arab horse societies in many countries.*

THOROUGHBRED

KEY FACTS

Color: most solid colors.
Height: from 14.2–17.2 hands, depending on purpose: average about 16 hands.
Physique: varies; refined head, long arched neck, sloping shoulder, deep chest, short strong back, deep body, muscular hindquarters, hard legs.
Character: bold, spirited.
Principal uses: racing, riding, cross-breeding.

THE THOROUGHBRED is famous the world over as the race-horse *par excellence*. It is the fastest, and the most valuable, horse in the world. However, it did not emerge as a breed until relatively recently.

Horse-racing, which had always been popular in England, reached new heights of popularity during the reign of Charles II. The fastest of the native mares, which probably included the now extinct Galloway ponies, had for some time been crossed with imported Arabs, Barbs and Turks, in order to improve the speed and performance of these "running horses," and gradually a better class of race-horse was emerging.

Although many Arab stallions were being used at this time, three in particular were very influential.

ANCESTRY

Arab
Turk
Barb
Galloway

Thoroughbred

The first to arrive in England was the Byerley Turk, which was put to stud in 1690. Next was the Darley Arabian, which arrived in 1704. Darley Arabian was the great-grandsire of Eclipse, the most famous race-horse of all time. Darley Arabian also sired Flying Childers, who was never beaten. The last was the Godolphin Arabian, which arrived in 1728.

These stallions were crossed with the best of the English racing mares so successfully that all Thoroughbreds registered in the General Stud Book, started in 1791, can be traced back to them. It is interesting that none of these stallions had themselves been raced. The popularity of Arab blood was probably due to the fact that it provided quality and the ability to breed true to type.

As horse-racing developed into an industry, breeders began to pay great attention to pedigree, and to use only horses that had proved themselves on the race-track. In the beginning, Thoroughbreds were raced over long distances of about 4 to 12 miles (6.4 to 19.3 km), but gradually demand grew for shorter races so that horses could be raced at a younger age. They became better fed and looked after, and as a result the breed became taller and faster, until it reached its peak in about 1850. Since then the Thoroughbred has changed little.

Foreign interest in the Thoroughbred has always been strong, and it has been exported in large numbers. It is now bred all over the world, and several countries are famous for producing top-class

TYPES OF THOROUGHBRED

Thoroughbreds are divided into those that race on the flat and those that race over jumps.

There are three categories of flat racers: the sprinters, which race over a distance of 5-7 furlongs (1,100-1,590 yd/1,000-1,450m) – these are young horses that mature early, and have a lot of speed but little stamina; middle-distances horses, which race over the "classic" distances of 1-1¾ miles (1.6-2.8 km), such as the Kentucky and Epsom Derbies; and the stayers, late-maturing horses that race over longer distances.

Those that race over jumps are divided into steeple-chasers and hurdlers. They require toughness, stamina and jumping ability.

Horses are bred for a specific category as each has different requirements.

horses. In particular, the United States is known for its outstanding young sprinters, and France for its middle-distance horses and stayers. Ireland also breeds consistently top-class Thoroughbreds.

The Thoroughbred, with its good conformation, long, easy action, and good balance, also provides a perfect riding horse. Crossed with horses with a calmer temperament, it produces excellent show-jumpers, event horses and hunters and it has been used in the creation or development of many modern breeds of sports horses, such as the Anglo-Arab, the Hanoverian, the Trakehner, and the Westphalian.

QUARTER-HORSE

THE QUARTER-HORSE is the oldest surviving American horse breed, although it was not officially recognized as a breed until 1941.

In the 17th century, on Sundays and holidays, the settlers of Virginia and the Carolinas used to enjoy racing their horses down the main street of the local town – usually a distance of about a quarter of a mile (0.4 km). Horses that had been bred by crossing local Chicasaw Indian ponies (mustangs of Arab, Barb and Turk origins) with Thoroughbreds imported from England proved extremely fast over this distance, and were soon in demand as breeding stock. Among these, a stallion called Janus, imported from England in 1756, is recognized as the foundation stallion of the breed. Janus had raced over 4 miles in England; however, his offspring were very successful over a quarter-mile.

Soon the Quarter-Horse was being carefully bred to produce a very fast horse with great powers of acceleration for sprint racing. With the development of Thoroughbred racing, quarter-mile racing also became more organized and more popular.

The breed quickly came to be valued for other qualities as well as its speed. It is a tremendously strong horse with very powerful shoulders and hindquarters, and it was able to carry heavy men and packs for long distances. It is able to make quick starts and tights turns, which make it the perfect horse for roping and cutting work with cattle. In addition it seemed to have a good instinct for cattle-work. It was taken west with the pioneers, and proved to be the ideal horse for working on the big ranches that were springing up across the country.

The modern Quarter-Horse combines strength, speed and agility with intelligence, and is also easily broken and handled, making it extremely popular. There are different types of Quarter-Horse depending on what type of work they have been for, but they all share the same Quarter-Horse qualities. The heavier type is produced for stock-work, and a

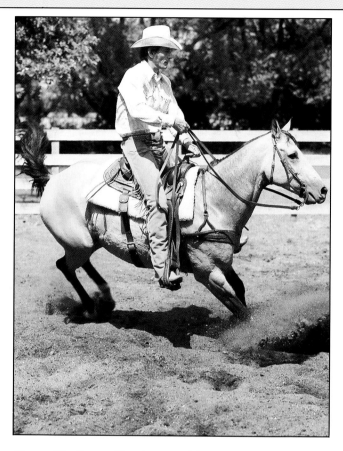

Above: *The Quarter-Horse's powerful hind-quarters enable it to move fast and low when it is working with cattle, starting and stopping suddenly and making tight turns. It is also kind, willing, docile and intelligent, and is the most popular horse breed in the United States today.*

THE RACING QUARTER-HORSE

The Quarter-Horse, named after the distance over which it excels, is still bred for racing, and the richest horse-race in the world is the All American Futurity for 3-year-old Quarter-Horses.

Despite the challenge provided by the Thoroughbred, the Quarter-Horse is still the fastest horse in the world over a quarter-mile (0.4 km), the current record being around 20 seconds.

lighter type for racing. To see a cutting horse at work, springing into a gallop from a standing start, skidding to a halt, and turning on a sixpence, is an exhilarating spectacle. Working cattle, it moves fast and low, anticipating every move that the calf makes.

The versatility of the Quarter-Horse is illustrated by the many types of class in which it is shown, such as working classes, jumping, hunting and polo classes. It is also successful in open classes against other breeds.

The Quarter-Horse is the most numerous breed in the United States today, with 2 million registered there. Its popularity has led to its being exported all over the world, and a further 800,000 are registered worldwide. It is now bred in Canada, South America, Australia, England and South Africa.

Above: Dash For Cash, the top money-winning Quarter-Horse in the US. Quarter-Horse racing has retained its popularity in the US despite the emergence of the Thoroughbred.

KEY FACTS

Color: solid colors, usually chestnut.
Height: 14.3–15.1 hands.
Physique: short head, muscular neck, short-coupled body, broad powerful hindquarters, fine legs.
Character: intelligent, versatile.
Principal uses: riding, ranch-work, rodeos, racing.

ANCESTRY

Arab
Barb
Turk
Andalusian
Thoroughbred

Quarter-Horse

MUSTANG

THE MUSTANG IS the feral horse of North America, descended from the horses of the Spanish settlers, and therefore of Andalusian, Arab and Barb origins. Mustangs roamed free for over 300 years, during which time they developed into hardy, thrifty, independent horses. Many were caught by the Indians, and later they were popular with the cowboys. Early Mustangs showed their Spanish and Barb origins, but many of the best were captured and the quality of the herds left in the wild declined.

The Mustang was found to have good cow-sense, and as well as being used for cattle-work, it was crossed with other larger breeds brought over by the early settlers to create larger working horses, and later with the Thoroughbred. The Quarter-Horse was the outstanding breed produced from the Mustang, and it was also influential in the development of the other stock breeds, the Appaloosa, Palomino and Pinto.

Today the wild Mustang has declined in numbers and is protected by law. In addition, various registries have been established to preserve the different blood-lines. The Spanish Mustang Registry is for

KEY FACTS

Color: all colors.
Height: 14–15 hands.
Physique: varies; lightweight build, hard legs and feet.
Character: independent, intractable.
Principal uses: stock-work, riding, endurance riding.

horses of obvious Barb descent. These horses are very good for general and endurance riding. The Spanish Barb Mustang Registry is for horses that are not of pure Barb descent but which still show the correct characteristics. There is also an American Mustang Association.

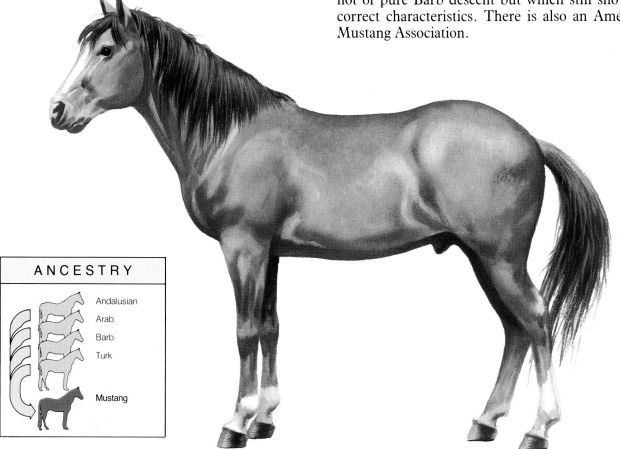

ANCESTRY

Andalusian
Arab
Barb
Turk

Mustang

MORGAN

ANCESTRY

Welsh Cob
Thoroughbred
Native Stock

Morgan

KEY FACTS

Color: predominantly bay, also brown, black, chestnut.
Height: 14–15 hands.
Physique: medium-sized head, slightly concave face, thick neck, deep chest, broad back, muscular quarters and high-set tail, legs set square.
Character: good-natured, hard-working, active.
Principal uses: general riding, harness work.

THE MORGAN is the first American breed. It was founded from a single stallion called Figure, foaled in Massachusetts in 1793, which eventually came to be named after one of its owners, Justin Morgan of Vermont. The origins of this stallion are unknown, but it is thought to be a combination of Welsh cob, Thoroughbred and native stock of Arab and Barb descent. Justin Morgan (the horse) excelled at both saddle and harness racing, and at pulling heavy weights, as well as being a good riding and ranch horse, and he was in great demand as a sire. He stamped his size, conformation and character on his offspring with such consistency that by the time of his death in 1821 a new breed had been created.

During the 19th century the Morgan was itself used in the foundation of other great American breeds, including the Standardbred, the Saddlebred and the Tennessee Walking Horse.

In the past the Morgan was used mainly for ranch and harness work, and proved its strength by doing heavy draft work. However, it is now also frequently used as a saddle horse.

With its strength and stamina, elegant high-stepping action and good nature, the Morgan is still popular today. It makes an ideal family horse as it takes easily to any form of equestrian activity, be it pleasure riding, endurance riding, or showing in harness.

APPALOOSA

FROM THE EVIDENCE of early cave paintings such as those as Lascaux, it appears that spotted horses existed as far back as prehistoric times. They are known to have existed in ancient Persia, and in China, and they appear again in Egyptian art. Spotted horses, probably descended from those of ancient Persia, were bred in Spain from about AD 100, and developed into a fine riding horse.

These horses were amongst those taken by the Spanish Conquistadores to Mexico in the 16th century, and are presumed to have escaped and spread across North America. The Nez Percé Indians of north-western America (now Washington, Oregon and Idaho) were skilled at horse-breeding, and from these escaped horses they produced spotted horses that were fast, strong and agile to cope with the mountainous terrain of the region, yet also docile and easy to handle. The Nez Percé Indians lived near the Palouse River and the breed came to be known as the *A Palouse*, and later the Appaloosa.

In 1877 the Nez Perce tribe was nearly destroyed by the US army. However, their horses were captured, and subsequent careful breeding has produced a spotted horse that in 1938 was recognized as a distinct breed. Although it is still found mainly in the western part of the country, it is now among the half-dozen most popular breeds in North America.

There are six main Appaloosa patterns, but no two horses are exactly the same. *Leopard* consists of an all-over white background with dark spots. *Snowflake* consists of an all-over dark background with white spots. *Spotted blanket* consists of a mainly dark

ANCESTRY

Andalusian
Arab
Barb
Turk

Appaloosa

Left and below: Six main Appaloosa patterns are recognized. The Appaloosa can be any color, but the markings must conform to one of these six patterns, such as the leopard pattern (left) and the spotted blanket (below).

KEY FACTS

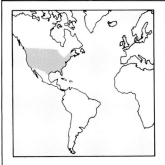

18
16
14
12
10
8
6
0

Color: six basic color patterns – frost, leopard, snowflake, marble, spotted blanket and white blanket.
Height: 14.2–15.2 hands.
Physique: short-coupled, thin mane and tail, hard feet which are often striped.
Character: courageous, docile.
Principal uses: pleasure riding, cow pony, parade and circus horse.

body, with dark spots on white back and/or hindquarters. *White blanket* consists of a mainly light body with dark back and/or hindquarters. *Marble* consists of a dark coat at birth that fades almost to white as the horse grows older, except for a few darker markings on legs and face. *Frosted tip* consists of a dark background with light-colored or white spots on loins and hips. There are several pattern variations. Roan is the most common ground color, although any color is acceptable, as long as the pattern conforms to an accepted one.

The Appaloosa has a smooth action and is tractable in character, making it popular as a general riding horse, and for trail-riding, driving and ranchwork. It is admired around the world for its distinctive appearance, and it is also in demand for shows and circuses.

Spotted horses and ponies exist all over the world. However, they are a breed, not a type, and they should not be confused with the Appaloosa.

STANDARDBRED

IN THE MIDDLE of the 19th century cross-breeding produced one of America's greatest breeds, the Standardbred, which today is the fastest harness-racing horse in the world.

The breed can be traced back to a Thoroughbred stallion called Messenger which was imported to the United States in 1788. Harness-racing was popular at that time, but it was an amateur affair, and no thought had been given to founding a breed of trotters. However, when Messenger was crossed with the fastest of the local harness-racers, horses resulted that had exceptional trotting speed. He

ANCESTRY

Thoroughbred
Canadian Trotter
Hackney
Narrangansett Pacer
Arab
Barb
Morgan

Standardbred

sired four sons to which almost all Standardbreds can be traced. As harness-racing became more popular during the 19th century, selective breeding was practiced to produce faster trotters. Thoroughbreds were crossed with more robust strains that had a talent for trotting, such as Canadian Trotters, Hackneys, Narragansett Pacers, horses of Arab and Barb origins, and Morgans.

The most famous and successful of Messenger's descendants, his great-grandson Hambletonian 10, born in 1849, sired over 1,300 offspring. He is regarded as the father of the modern Standardbred.

Harness-racing is divided into trotting and pacing. In both, the horse pulls a sulky (a light, two-wheeled vehicle) and is guided by a driver. Trotters move diagonally, in a conventional trot. Pacers move laterally, that is, the legs on the same side move together. Pacing is a natural gait, and horses born with a talent for pacing are trained for it from an early age. Many pacers wear hobbles, which synchronize their strides and prevent them from breaking the trot.

In 1871 the American Trotting Register was founded, and in 1879 a standard was laid down for inclusion in it. Over a distance of 1 mile (1.6 km) trotters had to attain a time of 2 minutes 30 seconds, and pacers a time of 2 minutes 25 seconds. It is from this standard that the breed takes its name.

Harness-racing is a popular sport in many coun-

tries around the world, and it is found in Australia, New Zealand, South Africa, and several European countries such as Sweden, Germany, France and Russia. It has been used to improve many trotting breeds, including the German Trotter, the French Trotter and the Orlov Trotter.

The Standardbred's conformation varies, as it has been bred primarily for speed. It resembles the Thoroughbred, but is heavier and more robust, and has very strong hindquarters. Although predominantly a harness-racing horse, the Standardbred's speed and stamina, keenness, and calm temperament make it excellent for general riding. Its qualities also suit it to endurance riding.

BREAKING THE RECORD

In 1871 the standard for the breed was set: 1 mile (1.6 km) in 2 minutes 30 seconds for trotters and 2 minutes 25 seconds for pacers. Yet this time had already been bettered in 1845, when 1 mile was trotted in 2 minutes 29½ seconds by a mare owned by Lady Suffolk. Nearly 100 years later, in 1938, the record stood at 1 mile trotted in 1 minute 55¼ seconds by a gelding called Grayhound. Recently the time for a trotter fell to 1 minute 54⅕ seconds.

Pacers are even faster than trotters, and the fastest recorded time over 1 mile by a pacer, achieved by a horse called Steady Star is 1 minute 52 seconds, the equivalent of 32 mph (

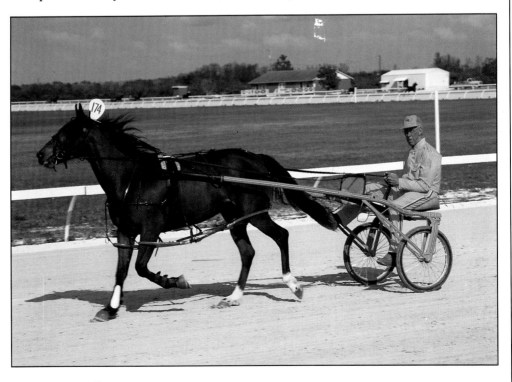

Right: *A pacer performing at Palm Beach, Florida. A pacer moves with lateral rather than diagonal strides, and can go slightly faster than a trotter. Horses with a natural inclination to pace are trained to it from an early age.*

SADDLEBRED

THE SADDLEBRED WAS DEVELOPED in Kentucky during the 19th century by plantation owners, who were looking for a horse that provided a comfortable ride for plantation work combined with a stylish, eye-catching action in harness. By crossing the best of their original stock of Thoroughbreds, Morgans and Narragansett Pacers, they produced a horse that was intelligent and responsive and which also had speed and stamina. With its high head-carriage and high-stepping action it is extremely elegant.

Intensive breeding has enhanced the Saddlebred's conformation and action, and it is now a very popular and successful show horse. The breed is divided into three divisions for showing. The Three-Gaited horse is shown in the three natural gaits. The Five-Gaited horse is shown in the three natural gaits and two man-made gaits, the slow gait and the rack. The slow gait is a very slow, smooth, four-beat movement. The legs, especially in front, are lifted very high. The rack is a fast version of the slow gait requiring a very snappy knee and hock action. The Fine Harness horse is shown with a four-wheel vehicle and is judged in two gaits, an animated walk and an airy part-trot.

Although it is best known as a show horse, the Saddlebred also makes a good general riding and driving horse.

KEY FACTS

Color: black, brown, bay, gray, chestnut.
Height: 15–16 hands.
Physique: narrow, refined head, large eyes, long elegant neck, sloping shoulders, short body, strong flexible hindquarters, long fine legs, high head and tail carriage.
Character: intelligent, gentle.
Principal uses: riding and showing.

ANCESTRY

Thoroughbred

Morgan

Narrangansett Pacer

Saddlebred

TENNESSEE WALKING HORSE

THE TENNESSEE WALKING HORSE (the Walker for short) was developed from the Thoroughbreds, Morgans, Standardbreds, Saddlebreds and Narragansett Pacers owned by the Tennessee settlers in the 18th century. Crosses of these led to the foundation stock of the modern breed.

In the beginning the Walker was intended as a general-purpose working horse, but its extreme comfort as a riding horse made it very popular with the owners of the vast southern plantations.

The Walker's conformation is unique. It has a compact and powerful frame. Its forelegs are set slightly apart, and its hindlegs are set with the hocks well away from its body. Its gaits – the flatfoot walk, running walk, and canter – have been developed specifically to produce a very smooth ride, and cannot be taught to any other breed. The flatfoot walk consists of a smooth, gliding action as the horse floats over the ground, its hind feet overstriding the front by 30–50 cm (12–20 in). The running walk is a faster version of this gait, in which the horse achieves great elevation, and can sustain a speed of up to 15 mph. In the canter it elevates its forehand with a rolling motion while its hindquarters remain almost level. The running walk is now inbred; foals are seen performing it just by copying their dams.

KEY FACTS

Color: chestnut, black, bay, roan; white markings common.
Height: 15–16 hands.
Physique: straight profile, long powerful neck, sloping shoulders and broad chest, short back, strong sloping hindquarters, legs fine, profuse tail carried high.
Character: docile, willing.
Principal uses: riding and showing.

ANCESTRY

Thoroughbred
Narrangansett Pacer
Morgan
Standardbred
Saddlebred

Tennessee Walking Horse

69

PALOMINO

ANCESTRY

Mustang

Palomino

KEY FACTS

18
16
14
12
10
8
6

0

Color: Gold, with light mane and tail; white markings allowed on legs.
Height: varies; usually over 14 hands.
Physique: varies; should be of riding horse/pony type.
Character: varies.
Principal uses: pleasure and trail riding, ranch-work, rodeos.

THE DISTINCTIVE AND BEAUTIFUL color of the Palomino has made it popular all over the world. It is defined by its color rather than its conformation, and as it does not breed true to type, it is not recognized as a breed except in the United States. Elsewhere it is registered as a type, and Palomino societies and stud books exist.

The Palomino's origins are believed to go back to ancient China, where the early emperors are reputed to have ridden golden horses. However, they reached America from Spain along with the early Spanish settlers. When the Spanish were defeated and their horses escaped, the Palominos gradually joined up with the herds of wild mustangs roaming North America. Later, they were picked out from these herds of wild horses, and became a popular mount of the cowboys.

The color of the Palomino should be that of a newly-minted gold coin, although in the United States slightly lighter and darker shades are also allowed. The mane should be white.

In North America the Palomino has been bred as a quality riding horse, and is used extensively for trail riding, stock work and rodeos. In Britain Palomino ponies are popular mounts for children.

The Albino is another color type that is recog- nized in the United States, where it has been bred since the early 20th century. It is probably de- scended from an Arab-Morgan stallion, and has bred true to type over several generations.

PINTO

THIS SPECTACULARLY-COLORED horse was traditionally associated with the American Indians. However, today it is popular for general pleasure riding and showing. Like the Palomino, the Pinto was originally registered as a color.

Pinto coloring falls into two types. Overo coloring consists of large bold patches of black with white. Tobiano coloring consists of white with smaller patches of any other color except black.

Today, three registers cover the Pinto in the United States, relating to different categories of conformation. The American Paint Horse Registry covers the Stock Horse type, for horses originally of Quarter-Horse or Thoroughbred breeding and conformation. The Association is dedicated to upgrading the Paint Horse, and to qualify horses must be of either Paint Horse, Quarter-Horse or Thoroughbred parentage. The Pinto Registry covers Pinto-colored horses of all breeds and types and has three divisions: the Stock Horse type; the Hunter type, an English horse of Arabian or Morgan origins; and the Saddle type, also an English horse, of Saddlebred origins. The Moroccan Spotted Horse Association covers gaited horses, such as those of Hackney, Tennessee Walking Horse, Morgan and Thoroughbred origins.

KEY FACTS

Color: black with white, or white with any color except black.
Height: varies.
Physique: varies.
Character: varies.
Principal uses: pleasure riding, ranch-work, showing.

ANCESTRY

Mustang

Pinto

FALABELLA

Left: At under 7 hands high, the Falabella is the smallest horse in the world. It was originally developed from a cross between a small Thoroughbred and a small Shetland. They are often kept as pets and are sometimes driven in harness, but they are not suitable for riding.

ANCESTRY

Shetland Pony
Thoroughbred
Falabella

AT A MAXIMUM HEIGHT of 34 in (86 cm) the Falabella is the smallest horse in the world. It is named after the Falabella family on whose ranch near Buenos Aires the breed has been developed.

The Falabella is known to be descended from a small Thoroughbred that was crossed with Shetlands to produce exceptionally small horses, but beyond that its origins are unclear. The genes producing the small size are still dominant today. Crossed with any mare a Falabella will produce a foal much smaller than the mare, and over a few generations a pony's descendants will shrink down to Falabella size.

The Falabella is a miniature horse, not a pony, and needs to be looked after as carefully as a Thoroughbred. The downgrading in size has reduced its strength so that it is not capable of carrying a rider. However, it is popular as a harness pony, and is also widely kept as a pet.

KEY FACTS

Color: all colors.
Height: under 7 hands.
Physique: proportioned like a miniature horse; fine bones and small feet.
Character: gentle and courageous.
Principal uses: harness pony and pet.

CRIOLLO

THE MODERN CRIOLLO, the native horse of Argentina, has developed from Andalusians, Barbs and Arabs brought over by the Spanish and which subsequently escaped. During the time that they ran wild on the Argentinian pampas plains, natural selection and adaptation to the rough conditions and extremes of temperature of this environment produced an exceptionally hardy breed.

The breed is quick, agile and intelligent and made an excellent cattle horse, becoming the favourite mount of the Argentinian gauchos.

Attempts to improve the Criollo by crossing with other breeds have not been successful, and today the Argentinians follow a program of selective breeding. The best animals from which to breed are chosen by an annual ride of 470 miles (750 km), carrying 238 lbs (108 kg) in weight, during which they may not be fed.

The Argentinian polo pony has been developed by crossing the Criollo with Thoroughbred stock, the Criollo providing stamina and toughness, and the Thoroughbred speed. Breeds such as the Crioulo in Brazil and the Llanero in Venezuela are also closely related to the Criollo, having developed in much the same way from similar Spanish stock. They now vary quite considerably from the basic Criollo type.

KEY FACTS

Color: dun with dark points and dorsal stipe; sometimes roan, chestnut, bay.
Height: 14 hands.
Physique: short, broad head, muscular neck, strong shoulders and broad chest, deep body, fine strong legs, small feet.
Character: tough, willing, great endurance.
Principal uses: riding and stock-work.

ANCESTRY

Andalusian

Barb

Arab

Criollo

PERUVIAN PASO

THE PERUVIAN PASO is the best known of the South American Paso breeds that developed from the Andalusians, Barbs and Spanish Jennets brought over by the Spanish Conquistadores.

The Peruvians needed a horse that could carry them comfortably for long distances over very rough and mountainous terrain, and they developed the breed carefully for over 300 years. The distinctive feature of the Peruvian Paso, as with the other Paso breeds, is its *paso* gait, which it is thought to have inherited from the Spanish Jennets. This is a lateral four-beat gait, in which the forelegs swing in an arc while the hindlegs take long, straight strides; the hindleg touches the ground fractionally ahead of the front leg. This produces a smooth, ambling pace that the horse can sustain for many miles at an average speed of about 11 mph.

The demands of working over long distances in the high Peruvian mountains gradually produced animals that were tough with great stamina. When breeding from them, the Peruvians looked for horses with a good *paso* gait, and also for those that were both proud and docile. This careful selection has produced a breed that is both tough and hardy, and exceptionally easy to break and handle. It is gaining popularity around the world due to its comfortable, easy gait and excellent temperament.

KEY FACTS

Color: bay, chestnut, brown, black, gray.
Height: 14.2–15.2 hands.
Physique: long crested neck, deep broad chest and body, strong fine legs, full mane and tail, high head carriage.
Character: docile, great endurance.
Principal uses: riding and stock-work.

ANCESTRY

Andalusian

Barb

Spanish Jennet

Peruvian Paso Horse

PASO FINO

KEY FACTS

Color: all colors.
Height: 14.3 hands.
Physique: Arab-type head, strong back and quarters, hard fine legs.
Character: spirited, tractable.
Principal uses: riding and stock-work.

THE PASO FINO of Puerto Rico is derived from the same origins as the Peruvian Paso.

It exhibits three *paso* gaits: the *paso fino*, performed at the pace of a slow walk; the *paso corto*, performed at the speed of a collected trot, at which it can cover very long distances; and the *paso largo*, performed at the speed of a slow canter.

Apart from the adaptations that the breed has made to the climate and conditions of South America, it is thought to be very similar to the original horses of the Spanish settlers.

In the United States, the American Paso Fino Horse Association is working towards merging the best characteristics from the various Paso breeds of Peru, Puerto Rico, Brazil, Venezuela and the Dominican Republic, to create an ideal Paso type.

ANCESTRY

Andalusian

Barb

Spanish Jennet

Paso Fino

GALICENO

THE GALICENO IS DESCENDED from ponies of the Galicia region of Spain that were among those taken over to the New World by the Spanish Conquistadores. These were probably Garrano ponies, but might have included Minhos from northern Portugal as well. These horses accompanied the Spanish when they conquered Mexico, and it is there that the Galiceno breed developed, although more through natural selection than by selective breeding on the part of man.

Through the Garrano the Galiceno contains a fair amount of Arab blood, and shows many characteristics of the Arab. It is intelligent, tough, full of stamina, and has a kind, gentle temperament. It has the appearance of a small, narrow-framed horse, and has an unusual extra gait – a fast running walk – which makes it a comfortable ride over long distances. In its native Mexico it is used for ranch-work and light transport work.

In 1959 Galicenos were first imported into the United States, and it has been very popular there. It learns quickly and has proved to be very versatile. It is used there for ranch-work and as a competition horse.

KEY FACTS

Color: bay, black, dun, sorrel, gray.
Height: 12-13.2 hands.
Physique: intelligent head, straight shoulders, narrow chest, short back, fine legs, small feet.
Character: alert, kind, intelligent.
Principal uses: ranch-work, transport.

ANCESTRY

Garranos

Galiceno

MANGALARGA

THE MANGALARGA BREED of Brazil is about 100 years old, and is the result of crossing Crioulo mares with Andalusian and Altér Real stock.

This resulted in a fine riding horse which has a distinctive fifth gait between trot and canter, called the *marcha*, that produces a comfortable rocking movement.

The Campolino, also from Brazil, is a heavier version of the Mangalarga.

KEY FACTS

Color: bay, chestnut, roan, gray.
Height: 15 hands.
Physique: longish head, short back, powerful hindquarters, low-set tail, long legs.
Character: hardy, great powers of endurance.
Principal uses: riding, stock-work.

ANCESTRY

Crioulo
Andalusian
Altér Real

Mangalarga

EXMOOR

ANCESTRY

Celtic Pony

Exmoor Pony

THE EXMOOR IS THE OLDEST of all the British native breeds. It is thought to have existed in prehistoric times and was probably the pony that pulled the chariots of the Celts. The Exmoor area is quite isolated and the breed has remained remarkably pure. In fact, evidence suggests that the modern pony has changed little from its early ancestors.

The moorland environment is harsh and solitary, and in response the Exmoor has developed the toughness and resilience for which it is renowned. It can even endure winters that bring several feet of snow, without shelter or additional feed being provided by man. The Exmoor is also extremely strong; it can even carry adult farmers for a day's hunting or shepherding.

Exmoors still run wild in herds, but they are privately owned and registered in a stud book. The ponies are rounded up once a year and driven down to the farms for inspection. Those accepted as good specimens of the breed are branded and registered.

The Exmoor's qualities of hardiness and endurance have made it very popular as foundation breeding stock; it produces particularly good stock when crossed with Thoroughbreds. In recent years Exmoor ponies have been exported all over the

KEY FACTS

Color: bay, brown or mouse dun; mealy muzzle; must not include white.
Height: mares up to 12.2 hands; stallions and geldings up to 12.3 hands.
Physique: broad forehead, thick neck, deep chest, short clean legs, hard feet.
Character: intelligent, quick-witted, alert, kind.
Principal uses: riding, foundation stock.

world for this purpose.

Although ponies taken off the moor seem wild at first, they make excellent children's riding ponies if they are well trained.

DARTMOOR

ANCESTRY

Celtic Pony

Dartmoor

DARTMOORS HAVE ROAMED the desolate moorland of southern Devon for many centuries. They are closely related to the Exmoor and are probably descended from the same stock. They have developed the same qualities of hardiness and surefootedness in response to their environment.

The earliest record of the breed appears in the will of Bishop Aelwold of Crediton in 1012. It is known that during the tin-mining era on Dartmoor, the ponies were used to carry the tin down from the moors. Once the mines closed, however, they were left to roam free again.

For some time Dartmoors were crossed with other breeds, resulting in great variations in type. However, the formation of a breed society, and the setting down of entry requirements, at the end of the 19th century has gone a long way towards stabilizing the breed. Since that time, considerable progress has been made in producing a first-class children's riding pony; the breed is now also valued as foundation stock for larger all-round ponies.

The Dartmoor pony is reliable and sensible. It is also extremely versatile: it goes well over jumps, and can be used for hunting and in harness. Its high head carriage and broad shoulders make children who are

KEY FACTS

Color: bay, brown, black.
Height: up to 12.2 hands.
Physique: small head, very small ears, strong neck, shoulders set well back, strong hindquarters, high-set full tail, slim, hard legs.
Character: quiet, reliable, kind, sensible.
Principal uses: excellent child's first pony.

learning to ride feel particularly safe on it, and this, coupled with its kind temperament and comfortable action, makes it an ideal first pony for children.

FELL

THE FELL PONY INHABITS the uplands of Cumbria on the western side of the Pennine Hills. It is thought to be descended from the Celtic pony, but has also been influenced by the Friesian, and later by the Galloway pony. Friesian horses were brought over by the Frieslanders to help the Romans build Hadrian's Wall in AD 120. When they had finished, they left behind a large group of Friesian stallions which bred with the native ponies to produce the Fell, and its neighbor, the Dales. Since that time the Fell has remained quite isolated, and today it breeds truer to type, and is more easily recognized, than any other native breed apart from the Exmoor.

The Fell is famous for its great strength. During the time that it was used for carrying lead from the local mines to the coast; it was reputed to have carried loads of 220 lb (100 kg) for 30 miles or more day after day. It was also used on the North Country farms for heavy agricultural work and harness work as well as shepherding and general riding. And on days off, the farmers would enter their ponies in local trotting races.

The modern Fell is extremely strong, and has plenty of stamina, making it suitable for harness work, for competitive events such as endurance riding, and for pleasure riding and trekking.

KEY FACTS

Color: usually black; also brown, bay, gray; white markings on legs permitted.
Height: 13–14 hands.
Physique: alert head, long neck, muscular body, strong legs with feathering, mane and tail long and thick.
Character: hard-working, lively.
Principal uses: riding, driving, trekking.

ANCESTRY

Celtic Pony

Galloway

Friesian

Fell

DALES

KEY FACTS

Color: black or brown; white star permitted.
Height: 13.2–14.2 hands.
Physique: neat head, strong neck, powerful compact body, short legs, thick mane and tail, feathering on feet.
Character: sensible, quiet, hardworking.
Principal uses: riding, agricultural work, trekking.

THE DALES PONY is closely related to the Fell, being descended from Celtic and Galloway pony origins. It inhabits the eastern side of the Pennine Hills.

Like the Fell, the Dales pony is immensely strong. It was widely used for transporting lead from the local mines to the coast ports and as a general pack-horse. Since it could pull heavy loads, farmers found it extremely useful for all types of agricultural work. It also made a good riding horse, being surefooted and agile, and a fast trotter. In the 19th century, Dales mares were crossed with a Welsh cob called Comet, a champion in the local trotting races, in order to increase the overall speed of the breed, and all Dales can be traced back to this stallion.

With the advent of motorized transport, the breed's numbers declined markedly until in the 1950s it nearly became extinct. With the formation of the Dales Pony Society in 1963, however, both interest in the breed, and its numbers, have increased again.

It is an ideal pony for trekking; it is also good for general riding although, due to its strength, it is more suitable for an adult than a child.

Crossed with Thoroughbred blood, the Dales pony produces excellent jumpers and hunters.

ANCESTRY

Celtic Pony
Friesian
Galloway
Welsh Cob

Dales

NEW FOREST

THE ORIGINS OF the New Forest pony are probably similar to those of the Exmoor and Dartmoor, as the forest it inhabited 1,000 years ago would have spread as far as Devon and Somerset. The earliest record of the breed occurred in the 11th century, during the rein of King Canute: horses were noted to be running wild in the forest.

The area is less remote than those inhabited by other native ponies, and over the centuries groups of other breeds were turned loose there, with the result that the New Forest pony now shows a range of types. Deliberate attempts were made to up-grade the wild ponies from time to time. In 1852, for example, Queen Victoria allowed an Arab stallion to run loose in the Forest for eight years to breed with the native mares. More recently, Thoroughbreds have also been used, as have stallions of other native breeds.

The New Forest is the second-largest of the native ponies. It has a narrower frame than the others, which makes it well suited as a children's pony, although it is strong enough to carry adults as well. Its quality as a riding and harness pony has made it popular all over the world.

New Forest ponies still run wild in the forest, the

KEY FACTS

Color: any color except piebald or skewbald; white markings permitted.
Height: 12–14.2 hands.
Physique: large head, long sloping shoulder, short back with deep girth, hard legs and good feet.
Character: intelligent, willing, friendly, docile.
Principal uses: children's riding pony.

stallions being inspected for quality each year. The breed's long exposure to human visitors has caused it to lose much of its natural nervousness of people, and it is particularly tractable and docile.

ANCESTRY

Celtic Pony

Native Breeds

Thoroughbred

Arab

New Forest

CONNEMARA

THE CONNEMARA IS the only native pony breed of Ireland. It is an ancient breed, and has run free in the mountains of the west coast since prehistoric times.

Its origins are unclear, but it is thought to be descended from the same stock as the Highland, Shetland, Icelandic and Norwegian Fjord ponies. However, the Connemara is lighter and more athletic than the other native breeds, and has a pretty, almost Oriental look. One theory put forward to explain this is that the breed was crossed with Spanish Jennets shipwrecked in the Spanish Armada in 1588. It is also possible that Galway merchants trading with Spain in the 16th and 17th centuries imported some Spanish and Oriental horses, which subsequently escaped and bred with the wild native ponies.

Until recently the Connemara was used as a general-purpose animal. However, today it is principally valued as a children's riding pony. It has a free, fluent action and can perform in all areas of equitation from dressage to hunting. However, it has a particular talent for jumping; and crossed with Thoroughbred stock it has produced some highly successful competition horses. It has also undoubtedly contributed to the development of the Irish Half-bred.

KEY FACTS

18
16
14
12
10
8
6

0

Color: usually gray; can be black, brown, bay.
Height: 13–14 hands.
Physique: intelligent, well carried head, medium-length neck on sloping shoulders, deep compact body, short legs.
Character: intelligent, kind, sensible, tractable.
Principal uses: riding, jumping, driving.

ANCESTRY

Celtic Pony

Spanish Jennet

Arab

Thoroughbred

Connemara

SHETLAND

ANCESTRY

Celtic Pony

Shetland Pony

KEY FACTS

Color: black, bay, brown, chestnut, gray, part-colors.
Height: up to 10.2 hands.
Physique: small head, sloping shoulders, deep thick-set body, short back, short legs with some feathering, small open feet.
Character: independent, headstrong.
Principal uses: riding and harness pony, pet.

THE SHETLAND PONY comes from the Shetland Islands off northern Scotland, where it was isolated for nearly 2,000 years before being brought over to the mainland during the 19th century. The origins of the breed are not known, but it is thought to be descended from a "dwarf" Exmoor type.

During the centuries of isolation on the islands the breed remained completely pure. In the 19th century, however, its value as a pit pony was recognized, and many were taken from the Shetlands and put to work down the mines. As a result, it was bred for quantity rather than quality, and the breed deteriorated until the late 19th century, when breeding farms were created to re-establish a good Shetland type. It became the first native pony to have its own society, and the stud book was opened in 1890.

At a maximum height of 10.2 hands the Shetland is the smallest of the native breeds, yet relative to its size it is the strongest pony in the world. Until quite recently it provided the only form of transport on its native islands, pulling carts of peat (for fuel) and seaweed (for fertilizer).

Although its size makes it an ideal pony for small children, its headstrong and independent character demands firm, though kind, handling to keep it under control. However, it makes an excellent harness-pony, and its performances in harness are one of the highlights of many shows.

HIGHLAND

KEY FACTS

Color: dun, ranging from golden-blue to silver-blue with dorsal stripe; sometimes black, gray-black, or brown.
Height: 13–14.2 hands.
Physique: neat head, solid deep body, short strong legs, well-shaped hard hooves.
Character: docile, intelligent, sensitive, trusting.
Principal uses: riding and trekking.

THE HIGHLAND PONY of northern Scotland is probably descended from the same Celtic type as the Exmoor, and has subsequently been influenced by the now-extinct Galloway, and later by Arab blood.

It was originally divided into two strains which developed separately according to local conditions and requirements. The mainland strain, known as the Garron, was the larger of the two, and at 14.2 hands is the largest and strongest of the native breeds. The Western Isles strain averaged about 12.2 hands. However, cross-breeding has now more or less eliminated these distinctions.

The Highland pony was the traditional partner of the Scottish crofters, who used it as a general-purpose working pony. They were able to carry great weights, while working on the craggy and difficult terrain of the Scottish Highlands produced remarkable agility and surefootedness, creating the ideal pack-horse for the mountains. However, they are not built for speed, the walk and trot being their two natural gaits.

The Highland pony is still found mainly in Scotland, where it is used in many roles. The larger ones are used by deer-stalkers to bring the carcasses down from the mountains; they make good trekking ponies; and are used for tree-felling work and shepherding. The smaller ones make good children's riding ponies.

ANCESTRY

Celtic Pony

Galloway

Arab

Clydesdale

Highland Garron

WELSH PONIES

THE WELSH NATIVE PONIES are considered by many to be the prettiest of the British pony breeds. The Welsh Pony stud book is divided into four sections: A, B, C and D.

SECTION A

The Welsh Mountain Pony (section A) is the original, and smallest, of the Welsh breeds, and is probably descended from the Celtic pony. There are references to wild mountain ponies going as far back as Roman times, and Julius Caesar established a stud at Lake Bala, Merionethshire. Within the last two to three hundred years, two Arab stallions have been allowed to roam the Welsh Mountains to improve the native stock, and this probably accounts for the breed's Arab looks.

Because it has lived on the mountains for over 1,000 years, this breed has become tough, resilient, surefooted and quick. In addition, it combines all the best pony qualities – courage, endurance, intelligence and gentleness. It also has natural jumping ability. As a result, it makes an excellent children's pony, and many children's riding ponies today have

KEY FACTS

Color: any color except piebald or skewbald.
Height: not over 12 hands.
Physique: small head, concave face, crested neck, sloping shoulders, short back, tail set high, short legs, neat feet.
Character: intelligent, kind, brave, spirited.
Principal uses: riding, foundation stock for riding ponies.

some Welsh blood in them. In addition, it has a good trot and goes well in harness.

The Welsh Mountain Pony has always bred out in the mountains, ensuring the continuance of the breed's natural qualities, and breeders from around the world import fresh stock from Wales to replenish and improve their own breeding stock. The Welsh Mountain has been used as foundation stock for three other Welsh breeds.

ANCESTRY

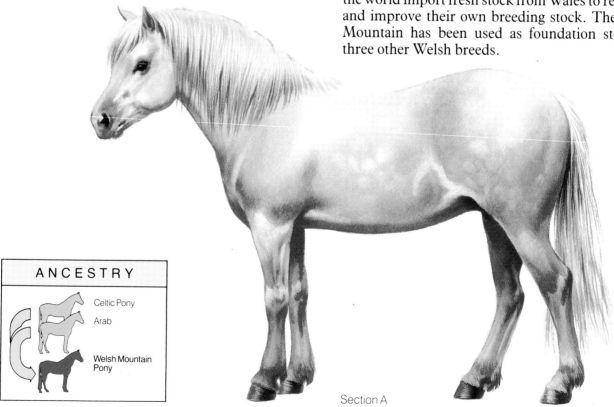

Celtic Pony

Arab

Welsh Mountain Pony

Section A

KEY FACTS

```
                    18
                    16
                    14
                    12
                    10
                     8
                     6
                     0
```

Color: as for Welsh Mountain.
Size: not over 13.2 hands.
Physique: as for Welsh Mountain; look for action, temperament and looks of quality riding pony.
Character: as for Welsh Mountain.

SECTION B

The Welsh Pony (section B) has been bred as a quality children's riding pony. It was created by crossing Welsh Mountain mares with a small Thoroughbred stallion called Merlin, a direct descendant of the Darley Arabian (see page 58), and these ponies are also known as Merlins. Arab and section C blood may also have been added. It is similar to the Welsh Mountain except that it is taller and more lightly built. It has retained all the pony characteristics.

SECTION C

The Welsh Pony (section C) is a smaller version of the Welsh Cob. It is energetic and brave, and very versatile. At one time it was used mainly in harness, although there is not much demand for it in that role now. However, it is ideally suited to the popular pastime of trekking as it can carry an adult comfortably. It is also a good hunting pony for a child.

SECTION D

The Welsh Cob (section D) is a larger version of the cob-type pony. It is thought to have been created around the 12th century, by crossing Welsh Mountain ponies with Spanish horses. It may also be related to the now extinct Old Welsh Cart-horse. During medieval times it was used as a pack-horse and for riding. Welsh Cobs are good trotters, and the breed has been used to create and improve trotting breeds around the world.

Section B

ANCESTRY

Welsh Mountain

Thoroughbred

Arab

Welsh Pony

CLEVELAND BAY

THE CLEVELAND BAY is probably the oldest of the British horse breeds. Its origins are thought to go back to a type of horse brought to Britain by the Romans. Certainly by medieval times, a type of pack-horse called the Chapman Horse was being used by travelling merchants, or "chapmen", in the north of England. It is from this horse that the Cleveland is descended.

The breed was developed in north-east England, where it was used as an all-rounder, for agricultural and draft work, in harness, and for riding and hunting. However, it was as a pack animal that the Cleveland was most valued, its strength and endurance enabling it to carry very heavy loads.

During the 19th century, owing to its strength, good looks and tractable nature, it became popular as a carriage-horse. At this time the breed received an injection of Thoroughbred blood, and the result was so popular that another breed with additional Thoroughbred blood, the Yorkshire Coach Horse, was created. This classy and fashionable carriage-horse became extinct in the 1930s.

It is as a carriage-horse that the Cleveland Bay excels today, and it is consistently successful in driving competitions. It also has natural jumping ability and, crossed with the Thoroughbred, produces international class jumpers and dressage horses.

KEY FACTS

Color: bay; a small star is allowed.
Height: 15.2–16 hands.
Physique: large head, long neck, long deep-girthed body, short strong clean legs.
Character: intelligent, sensible, calm, tractable.
Principal uses: driving, riding.

ANCESTRY

Native
Chapmen Horses

Thoroughbred

Cleveland Bay

HACKNEY

KEY FACTS

Color: bay, dark brown, black.
Height: 14–15.3 hands (horse); under 14 hands (pony).
Physique: small head with convex face, long neck, compact body with deep chest, short legs with strong hocks, tail set and carried high, fine silky coat.
Character: spirited, alert, courageous.
Principal use: driving.

THE DEVELOPMENT OF THE modern Hackney is well documented.

The Hackney Horse was created from the British regional breeds of trotters, the Norfolk and Yorkshire Trotters, which had been developed as fast-trotting harness horses. In the early 19th century, these two breeds were crossed to produce the lighter Hackney Horse. At this time proper roads were being built, and the Hackney, with its elegant, fast trotting gait and powers of endurance, provided a quick means of transport.

In the middle of the 19th century the Hackney Pony was created by crossing the Hackney Horse with Fell mares. The Hackney blood provided speed and elegance, the Fell power and a high knee-action. The Hackney Pony should look like a pony type, with a small, intelligent head, but it shares the features of spectacular action, high spirits and endurance with the Horse.

The special characteristic of the Hackneys is their action. At the trot they have a high, ground-covering knee action, the foreleg being raised up and thrown forward in an extravagant movement. They are a regular feature item in the show-ring, as well as being popular in competition classes.

ANCESTRY

Norfolk Roadster

Thoroughbred

Hackney Horse

SHIRE

THE SHIRE IS THE GREATEST of the heavy horse breeds, standing at up to 18 hands high, and weighing over a ton (approximately 1,000 kg).

The breed is probably descended from the Great Horses and Old English Blacks that were ridden into battle by the medieval knights. The ancestry of these breeds is uncertain but probably stems in part from the Friesian and Flanders horses of northern Europe.

The Old English Black was a popular draft horse, especially in the midland counties of England, in the 18th and 19th centuries. It was particularly in demand for transporting the raw materials and products of the Industrial Revolution.

During the mid-nineteenth century indiscriminate breeding to fill the demand for draft horses led to a deterioration in the quality of the breed, and in 1878 the Shire Horse Society (at first known as the Cart-Horse Society) was formed in order to raise and maintain standards again.

These marvellous, aristocratic horses are a pleasure to work with. Their popularity, and ability to draw large crowds at shows, has ensured the breed's survival despite the fact that it is no longer in demand as a working horse.

KEY FACTS

Color: black, bay, gray, with white markings.
Height: 16.2–17 hands; stallions can reach 18 hands.
Physique: slightly convex profile, wide chest, deep broad girth, dense muscular body, long legs with feathering.
Character: docile, gentle, kind, hard-working.
Principal uses: draft, showing.

ANCESTRY

Friesian
Old English Black Horse
Flanders Horse
Native Stock

Shire

SUFFOLK PUNCH

KEY FACTS

Color: chestnut, in seven shades – red, gold, copper, yellow, liver, light, dark.
Height: 16 hands.
Physique: large head, deep neck, massive shoulders, round compact body, clean legs, short cannon bone.
Character: gentle, active, docile.
Principal uses: draft, showing.

THE SUFFOLK PUNCH is the purest bred of the British heavy horses. All members of the breed can be traced to a trotting horse foaled in 1760, although the breed was mentioned in records as early as 1506.

It may be descended from the Great Horse, and in the 16th and 17th centuries Flanders stallions are known to have been put to Suffolk mares. In the 18th century attempts were made to introduce a smarter element into the breed by crossing it with Norfolk Trotter, Cob and even Thoroughbred blood.

The Suffolk Punch has many assets. It is very long-lived, often working well into its twenties, and living beyond the age of thirty. It can thrive on poor keep. Its large, broad shoulders and short legs give it tremendous pulling power. And it always breeds true to color – chestnut.

In earlier times the Suffolk was considered the best horse for agricultural work. Today, its personality and presence ensure that it is preserved for its own sake.

ANCESTRY

Native Great Horse

Flanders Horse

Norfolk Trotter

Cob

Thoroughbred

Suffolk Punch

IRISH DRAFT

ANCESTRY

Native Stock

Connemara

Thoroughbred

Irish Draft

THE IRISH DRAFT was created in the 18th century by crossing Thoroughbred stallions with native Irish mares. Its previous origins are unknown.

This cross-breeding resulted in a fine, powerful and versatile horse. It was strong enough for heavy agricultural work and carriage-driving. At the same time, it was an active horse with powerful hind-quarters, making it excellent for riding and hunting. The Irish Draft flourished until the agricultural recession in 1879. After that its numbers declined sharply until the Irish Government stepped in, in 1907, to help promote the interests of the breed. It was found that when crossed with the Thorough-bred, it produced excellent hunting and competition horses that were popular all over the world, and Ireland became a major exporter of these horses.

Today the number of pure-bred horses has declined badly, but the Irish Government is again taking action to restore the breed. There is also an effective Irish Draft Horse society working to preserve it.

KEY FACTS

Color: bay, brown, chestnut, gray.
Height: 15–17 hands.
Physique: intelligent head, short muscular neck, long powerful body, strong legs, very little feather.
Character: quiet, alert, sensible, willing.
Principal uses: hunting, cross-breeding for competition horses.

IRISH HALF-BRED

THE IRISH HALF-BRED, or Irish Hunter, was until recently classed as a type, and the breed is still being developed. It is produced by crossing a Thoroughbred with an Irish Draft. This has produced top-class competitive horses that are outstanding as show-jumpers and eventers.

Since the 1970s the Irish Horse Board has been overseeing the development of the breed. It still shows a variety of types, depending on the parentage, but the majority have good, alert heads and are strongly built.

KEY FACTS

Color: any solid color.
Height: 16.1 hands.
Physique: varies; classic hunting or show-jumping type.
Character: intelligent, bold, sensible.
Principal uses: hunting, show-jumping, eventing.

Left: The Irish Half-Bred has produced many top-class show-jumpers, such as Ryan's Son, seen here in action at Rotterdam.

ANCESTRY

Irish Draft
Thoroughbred
Connemara

Irish Halfbred

ANGLO-ARAB

KEY FACTS

Color: most solid colors.
Height: 16 hands.
Physique: delicate head, withers set well back, deep chest, short back, well-proportioned hindquarters, tail set high, long slender legs.
Character: brave, spirited, intelligent.
Principal uses: riding and competition.

ALTHOUGH THE ANGLO-ARAB, which is a cross between an Arab and a Thoroughbred, is found in many parts of the world, in France it has been developed as a distinct breed.

The French Anglo-Arab originated from English Thoroughbreds and pure-bred Arabs during the 1840s. In the beginning there were two strains, the southern part-bred and the pure-bred. The southern part-bred was developed in the Limousin area of south-west France by crossing Arabs or Thoroughbreds with native mares that were themselves of Arab or Oriental origins. The pure-bred Anglo-Arab was developed from direct crosses between Arab and Thoroughbred blood. Because the part-bred and pure-bred strains are now very similar in temperament and type, they have been combined in one stud book which is open to any horse resulting from a combination of English Thoroughbred, pure-bred Arab and Anglo-Arab as long as it has at least 25 per cent Arab blood.

The Anglo-Arab has excelled as a competition horse, and Anglo-Arab stallions have been used to up-grade the quality of other breeds, particularly the Selle Française, or French Riding Horse. This term covers the breed previously known as the Anglo-Norman, created by crossing local Normandy mares with Thoroughbred blood, together with other French pedigreed riding horses.

ANCESTRY

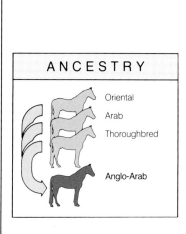

Oriental
Arab
Thoroughbred
Anglo-Arab

FRENCH TROTTER

ANCESTRY

Norfolk Trotter

Native Stock

Standardbred

French Trotter

KEY FACTS

Color: chestnut, bay, brown most common.
Height: 16.1 hands.
Physique: alert head, strong straight shoulders, short back, well-muscled powerful hindquarters, long hard legs with short cannon bone.
Character: willing, tough.
Principal uses: harness-racing, general riding, cross-breeding.

THE FRENCH TROTTER was developed principally in Normandy during the middle part of the 19th century. The first trotting course to open in France was at Cherbourg in 1836, and others sprang up soon afterwards. As the sport grew in popularity, so did the demand for good horses.

The early horses were produced by crossing good English trotting blood, usually Norfolk Trotters, with the Anglo-Norman to produce a strain of Anglo-Norman specially suited to the sport.

Later in the century these Anglo-Normans were further improved by the importation of foreign stallions, notably the Standardbred from America, which by that time had been developed into a very fast harness-horse.

In 1922 a stud book was opened for Anglo-Normans that had proved themselves by trotting one kilometre in 1 minute 42 seconds in a race. These horses came to be known as French Trotters, and the new breed was established.

CAMARGUE

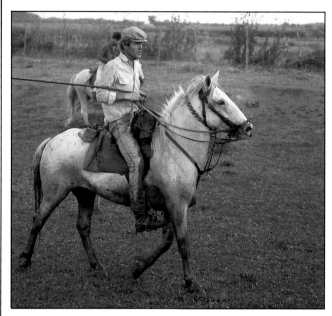

Above: *The Camargue is fast, agile and quick witted. It is the favorite mount of the* gardiens, *who use them for herding cattle, and in particular for rounding up the black bulls of the area.*

THESE FAMOUS HORSES, which have captured the imagination of horse-lovers all over the world, have roamed wild in the marshlands of the Camargue region, in the Rhône Delta of France, for many hundreds of years. Their origins are unknown but it is possible that they can be traced back to horses known to have lived in the area in prehistoric times. From their appearance it is very likely that they are in part descended from Arab and Barb horses brought to the area by the Romans and later the Moors.

The Camargue live on rough marsh grass and saltwater. In response to the climate and environment of the marshlands, they have developed into rugged, robust, surefooted horses.

The Camargue has a high-stepping walk, a fast gallop, and can twist and turn quickly. Although essentially wild, those that are caught and broken

ANCESTRY

Arab

Barb

Camargue

KEY FACTS

Color: gray.
Height: 13.2–14.2 hands.
Physique: large Oriental-type head with straight profile, short shoulder and back, slight hindquarters, fine legs, large feet.
Character: tractable when tamed.
Principal uses: herding and trekking; also roams wild.

Above: The Camargue is known as the White Horse of the Sea. It is an ancient breed, and its appearance suggests that it has Arab ancestry. It still runs wild in the marshlands of the Rhone Delta and has only recently been recognized as a breed.

make good riding horses. They are popular with the *gardiens* (Camargue cowboys) for herding cattle, and especially for rounding up the equally famous black bulls of the Camargue that are bred for bull-fighting. They are also used for pony-trekking in the Camargue area.

The Camargue has been officially recognized as a breed since 1968. There are about 30 herds in existence at the moment. Although the horses run wild and their breeding is not controlled, round-ups take place once a year and young stallions at about the age of three that are not of sufficient quality to be allowed to breed are removed and gelded. This has led to a notable improvement in the breed. The foals are born dark, and turn the characteristic gray color as they mature. They grow whiter as they age.

PERCHERON

THE PERCHERON IS the most famous and most numerous of the French draft horses, both in France and around the world. Its intelligent and docile nature inspire great enthusiasm and loyalty in its admirers, and much attention is paid to the quality and purity of the breed.

The breed originated in north-west France, in the Paris-basin area of La Perche, probably through the mixing of local Norman horses with Arabs and other Oriental breeds left behind in western Europe by the Moors. This produced a heavy horse that was used at first by the medieval knights. Subsequently the breed was crossed with heavier draft breeds to produce a very strong working horse. It is still used for agricultural work today, and is also popular in the show-ring.

An infusion of Arab blood in the 19th century contributed to the Percheron being active and lively. It also has great elegance for a heavy breed.

There is a smaller type of Percheron, known as the Postier Percheron.

The Boulonnais, another heavy draft breed from northern France, is descended in part from the same Oriental stock, together with Andalusian blood, and is very similar to the Percheron.

KEY FACTS

Color: gray or black.
Height: 15.2–17 hands.
Physique: straight profile, deep crested neck, deep powerful chest, short body, very powerful hindquarters, thick muscular legs, as little feathering as possible.
Character: active, intelligent, good-natured.
Principal uses: draught.

ANCESTRY

Oriental
Heavy
Draught Breeds
Norman

Percheron

DRAFT BRETON

KEY FACTS

Color: gray, chestnut, bay.
Height: 15–16 hands; Postier Breton not above 15 hands.
Physique: wide short head, strong neck, broad body, short muscular legs, a little feathering; Postier Breton lighter and more elegant.
Character: lively, intelligent, good-natured.
Principal uses: agricultural work, light draught.

THERE ARE TWO TYPES of Breton, the Draft Breton and the Postier Breton, both of which were developed in the Brittany area of north-west France.

The Draft Breton developed originally from the Roussin, a native of Brittany in the Middle Ages. The Roussin was a riding horse known for its comfortable, ambling fourth gait. When a heavier horse was needed for draft and agricultural work, the Roussin was crossed with the Percheron, the Ardennes (an ancient, gentle and particularly tough breed of draft horse from the Ardennes region of France and Belgium) and the Boulonnais (an active and lively draft breed from northern France), giving rise to the Draught Breton.

During the 19th century the Draught Breton was crossed with Norfolk Trotter and Hackney blood, creating the Postier Breton, a lighter, more elegant horse with a smart action that was used as a coach and light draft horse.

The Breton is still used today for agricultural work in Brittany, in the Midi vineyards, and in some of the Third World countries.

Today the two types of Breton have their own divisions within one stud book.

ANCESTRY

Native Stock

Percheron

Ardennes

Boulonnais

Draught Breton

FRIESIAN

KEY FACTS

Color: black only.
Height: 15 hands.
Physique: fine long head, crested neck, strong compact body, rounded hindquarters, short legs with feathering, very full mane and tail.
Character: quiet, willing, sensitive, hard-working, active.
Principal uses: driving.

THE FRIESIAN IS ONE of the oldest European horse breeds. Its origins are unknown, but a type of heavy horse is known to have existed in the Friesland region of the northern Netherlands over 3,000 years ago. The Friesian was popular with the Romans, who took it over to Britain where it contributed towards the development of the Fell and Dales ponies. It was popular with the knights of medieval times, and it appears in paintings by many of the Dutch Old Masters. By this time it had probably been crossed with the Andalusian, Arab and Barb.

The Friesian's outstanding feature is its very fast trot with a high knee-action. During the 19th century, it was used to improve other trotting breeds, such as the Orlov Trotter and the Norfolk Trotter (through which it influenced the Morgan).

The Friesian's popularity for cross-breeding, coupled with the decline in demand for working horses, caused its numbers to drop drastically before World War I, when action was taken to save the breed with the help of Oldenburg stallions (a breed originally derived from the Friesian).

The Friesian is easy to train, and has a spectacular action, making it successful as a competition and show carriage-horse, and in the circus-ring.

The Friesian was crossed with the Oldenburg and East Friesian to produce the Groningen, a slightly larger horse that is used for driving, riding and light draft-work.

ANCESTRY

Friesland Stock
Andalusian
Arab
Barb
Oldenburg

Friesian

BELGIAN HEAVY DRAFT

THE BELGIAN HEAVY DRAFT (also known as the Brabant), from the Brabant region of Belgium, has a very ancient lineage. It is thought to be a direct descendant of the Flanders Horse, one of the medieval war-horses in northern Europe.

Following the Reformation, other blood-lines were introduced in an attempt to change the Brabant, but they were not very successful, and ever since that time breeders have worked only with pure Brabant strains. The result is a magnificent horse that always breeds true to type.

It is one of the strongest of the heavy breeds, and has always worked as an all-round agricultural horse in Belgium. Its great strength and good nature have made it very popular, and it has been exported all over the world, especially to America. It has been used to found breeds of heavy horse, such as the Rhineland from Germany, and to improve other breeds of heavy horse, such as the Ardennes, whose size it has increased.

KEY FACTS

Color: most are red roan with black points; sometimes bay, brown, dun, gray.
Physique: square head relatively small, strong deep neck, powerful shoulders, short compact body, massive powerful hindquarters, short strong legs with some feathering.
Character: docile, willing, active, bold.
Principal uses: draft.

ANCESTRY

Flanders Horse

Belgian Heavy Draft

FRANCHES MONTAGNES

KEY FACTS

Color: most solid colors.
Height: 14.3–15.2 hands.
Physique: conformation varies; small head, compact body, strong legs, a little feathering.
Character: docile, energetic.
Principal uses: agricultural and army work.

THE FRANCHES MONTAGNES (also known as the Freiburger) is a light draft horse from the Jura Mountains of Switzerland. Its origins are a mixture of Norman, Anglo-Norman, Thoroughbred and draft breeds.

Having developed in the mountains, the Franches Montagnes is agile, strong, surefooted and full of stamina. It has been an invaluable working horse for the Swiss farmers, who have used it for all types of agricultural work until quite recently, and still use it on the higher fields that are too steep for a tractor. Its value is also recognized by the Swiss Army, who depend on it for transporting men and equipment quickly through the mountains.

Because of its importance to Swiss agriculture and defense, and because it is also seen as a good source of alternative energy and transport by the Swiss, the government controls the breeding program at the state-financed National Stud at Avenches. Because it is bred for character and ability rather than conformation, there is no fixed type.

The Franches Montagnes has also been used to develop a new breed, the Freiburger Saddle-Horse, by crossing it with the Shagya Arab. The Freiburger Saddle-Horse is an elegant riding horse with an excellent temperament.

ANCESTRY

Norman

Anglo-Norman

Thoroughbred

Draft Breeds

Franches Montagnes

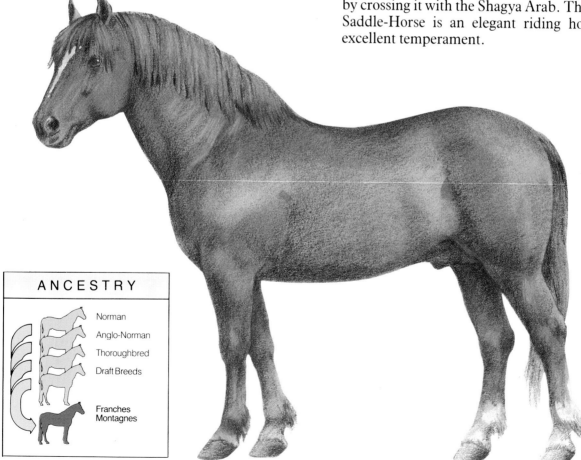

TRAKEHNER

KEY FACTS

Color: any solid color, usually dark.
Height: 16–16.2 hands.
Physique: elegant head, long neck, prominent withers, deep chest, strong medium-length back, rounded hindquarters, slender legs and good feet.
Character: tractable, spirited, courageous, versatile.
Principal uses: general riding, competition.

THE TRAKEHNER ORIGINALLY came from the area once known as East Prussia, now part of Poland. The breed was originally developed at the Trakehnen stud, which was established in 1732. The local Schwieken horses were used as foundation stock, and crossed with Thoroughbred and Arab blood to produce an elegant coach and cavalry horse.

The breed was badly depleted during World War II, and in the winter of 1945 about 700 Trakehner mares and a few stallions travelled west with refugees fleeing from the Russians. These horses were used to re-establish the breed in West Germany. It has been carefully nurtured since that time, and today is one of the most elegant of horses. It also breeds very true to type.

The Trakehner's good looks, free, extravagant action and versatility has made it popular as a show and dressage horse as well as for general riding.

The Trakehners that were left behind in Poland have been used to create the Wiekopolski breed. It was one of several breeds used to create the Wurttemburg, a good heavyweight riding and light draft horse. It has also been used to refine other breeds, such as the Hanoverian.

ANCESTRY

Schweiken
Arab
Thoroughbred

Trakehner

HANOVERIAN

MANY OF THE GERMAN BREEDS are defined according to the area that they come from, and the Hanoverian originates from Hanover in north-western Germany. Since it was created in the early 18th century, it has been altered quite considerably in order to adapt it for different uses at different times.

The breed was founded in 1735 by Royal decree at the Celle state stud. Holstein stallions were used to lighten the native mares descended from the Great War-Horse of the Middle Ages, to produce horses that were good for agricultural and coaching work. This process was continued by crossing with Thoroughbreds and Cleveland Bays imported from England and, towards the end of the 18th century, other imported breeds such as Andalusians.

In 1867 a breed society was formed with the aim of producing a horse equally suited to coach and military work and remarkable results were achieved. However, after World War I, horses were no longer needed in the same numbers by the military, and the breed society re-stated its aims: to produce a bold horse good for general farm, coach and riding work. From that time all stallions have been tested for speed, strength and endurance before being allowed to breed.

After World War II, the Hanoverian was no longer needed for farm-work or coach-work, and the society again re-stated its aims: to produce a riding horse of "superior performance." Thoroughbred, Trakehner and Arab blood has been used to refine the Hanoverian into a top-class, athletic, strong and good-tempered riding and competition horse.

Hanoverians have excelled in show-jumping, eventing and dressage competitions at international level, and the breed is now also widely used to upgrade the quality of other sports horses around the world.

ANCESTRY

Great War Horse
Holstein
Thoroughbred
Cleveland Bay
Andalusian
Trakehner
Arab

Hanoverian

KEY FACTS

Color: all solid colors.
Height: 15.3–17 hands.
Physique: varies; compact, powerful body, short strong legs.
Character: intelligent, sensible, willing, bold.
Principal uses: competition and general riding.

Above: Dynasty, ridden by Cynthia Ishoy, competing for Canada at the Olympic Games in 1988. This horse demonstrates the elegance, style, athleticism and supreme elegance characteristic of the Hanoverian.

The Hanoverian has also been used in the creation of new breeds. It has been crossed with Arab and Thoroughbred blood to produce the Westphalian, an excellent riding horse that is nearly as numerous in Germany as the Hanoverian.

The Hanoverian together with Thoroughbred and Trakehner blood, has created another excellent, athletic riding horse, the Danish Sport Horse, which is particularly successful in dressage competitions.

The Hanoverian is closely related to the Mecklenburg of East Germany, as similar blood-lines were used to create both breeds, and much cross-breeding has taken place between them. The Mecklenburg is the slightly smaller of the two, and is now bred as an all-round riding horse.

OLDENBURG

THE OLDENBURG HAS flourished in the north-west region of Germany since the 17th century.

The breed was based on the Friesian horses of the Netherlands. In the beginning, these heavy draft horses were crossed with Andalusians and Barbs to produce a lighter type of working horse, which was refined still further during the 19th century by crossing with Cleveland Bays, Thoroughbreds, Anglo-Normans and Hanoverians.

At this time, the breed was used as a high-class coach-horse. It was also used for agricultural work and by the military. After World War I, it was no longer needed by the army, but continued to be in demand as a farm-horse and coach-horse until World War II. When it was no longer needed as a working horse, breeders began to cross it with Thoroughbred and Trakehner blood, in order to refine and lighten the breed to make it suitable for all-round riding.

The Oldenburg, together with the Thorough-bred, Cleveland Bay and Norman, has been used to modify the old Rotteler draft breed to produce a riding horse that is now known as the Bavarian Warm-blood.

KEY FACTS

Color: any solid color; black, brown or bay most common.
Height: 16.2–17.2 hands.
Physique: plain head, straight profile, strong neck, muscular chest and body, strong hindquarters, short legs.
Character: bold, sensible.
Principal uses: riding, competition, driving.

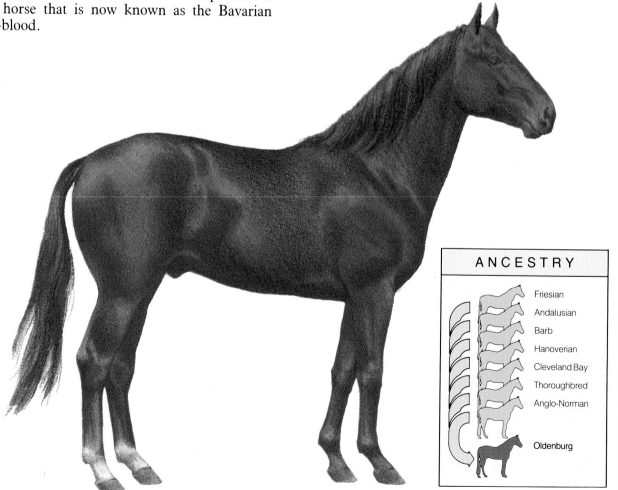

ANCESTRY

Friesian

Andalusian

Barb

Hanoverian

Cleveland Bay

Thoroughbred

Anglo-Norman

Oldenburg

EAST FRIESIAN

THE EAST FRIESIAN is from the East Friesland region of East Germany. The breed was developed from the Oldenburg, its close neighbor, and until World War II the two breeds were constantly exchanged and inter-bred.

However, since World War II the two breeds have been separated and have developed differently.

Cross-breeding with Arab and Hanoverian blood has refined and lightened the East Friesian, added strength and compactness, and given it a distinctive head. It has an excellent temperament, and is used as an all-round riding, competition and harness horse.

KEY FACTS

Color: any solid color.
Height: 15.2–16.2 hands.
Physique: similar to the Oldenburg but lighter, and with a more elegant head.
Character: bold, spirited, good-natured.
Principal uses: general riding, driving.

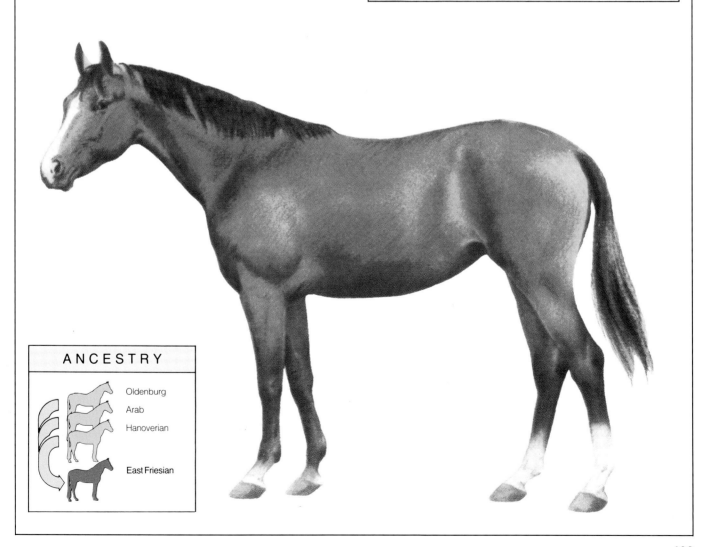

ANCESTRY

Oldenburg
Arab
Hanoverian

East Friesian

HOLSTEIN

KEY FACTS

Color: most solid colors.
Height: 16–17 hands.
Physique: elegant head, strong neck, powerful shoulders, deep girth, compact body, strong hindquarters, short legs.
Character: intelligent, willing, bold, versatile, good-natured.
Principal uses: general riding, competition.

THE HOLSTEIN IS probably the oldest of the German horse breeds. It comes from the marshlands of Schleswig-Holstein in northern Germany, and is known to have been bred there since the 14th century. In the beginning, Andalusians and Neapolitans were crossed with the local Marsh Horse (one of the Great Horse types) to produce a large, powerful horse that was popular all over Europe.

During the 19th century, the Holstein was crossed with Cleveland Bays and Thoroughbreds to refine the breed and produce a powerful carriage-horse with a high-stepping action and great stamina. The Cleveland Bay and Thoroughbred blood also contributed to the breed's jumping ability and talent for dressage.

The breed's numbers had dwindled by the end of World War II, and since that time great success has been achieved in building up and further refining the breed using Thoroughbred blood to produce top-quality competition horses.

Today the Holstein is successful in all areas of competitive riding at the highest level.

The Holstein is one of several breeds that have contributed to the Swiss Half-bred. This outstanding horse is powerful and athletic, and has a good temperament. It has been successful at the highest level.

ANCESTRY

Marsh Horse
Andalusian
Neapolitan
Cleveland Bay
Thoroughbred

Holstein

SCHLESWIG HEAVY DRAFT

THE SCHLESWIG WAS developed in the Schleswig-Holstein region of Germany during the 19th century to meet the heavy demand for horses for agricultural and draft work.

There were two major influences on the development of the breed: the Jutland, its neighbour in Denmark, which is thought to have been ridden by the Vikings, and which was certainly used as a warhorse by the Danes; and the Suffolk Punch from England. Other breeds, such as the Breton, Boulonnais (an elegant, active heavy draft horse from northern France), Cleveland Bay and Thoroughbred, have subsequently been used to correct faults in the breed, and have also had the effect of making it lighter and more lively.

It was used as an all-round heavy draft horse for industrial and agricultural work and by the army for moving artillery.

KEY FACTS

Color: usually chestnut with flaxen mane and tail.
Height: 15.1–16 hands.
Physique: large head with convex profile, short powerful neck, deep girth, long flat body, short muscular legs, a little feathering.
Character: willing, kind.
Principal uses: draft.

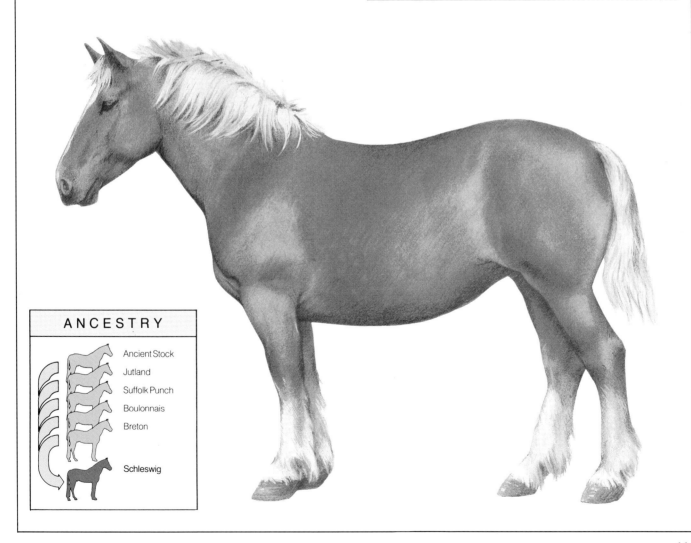

ANCESTRY

Ancient Stock
Jutland
Suffolk Punch
Boulonnais
Breton

Schleswig

LIPIZZANER

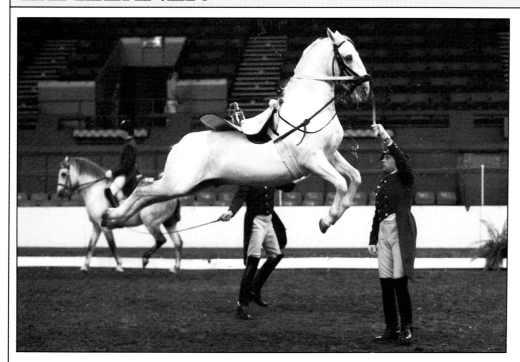

Left: A Lipizzaner stallion performs the Capriole, the most difficult of the Haute Ecole movements. All the movements taught at the Spanish Riding School date from the time when horses wre used in battle, and had the purpose of making the horse supple and agile so that it could evade an enemy quickly.

THE LIPIZZANER IS Austria's most celebrated horse, known the world over for its displays of high-school dressage with the Spanish Riding School of Vienna.

The Lipizzaner was first bred at Lipizza stud (now in Yugoslavia) by Archduke Charles of Austria. High-school equitation was fashionable in the courts of Europe at the time and he wanted horses that would excel at it. In 1580 he imported Andalusian stallions, which were considered best for high-school equitation, and crossed them with local mares.

Over the next 300 years, other breeds were also imported and crossed with the stock – notably the Neapolitan (an Italian breed, now extinct, produced by crossing Andalusians with Arab and Barb blood), Kladrubers and Fredericksborgs (both also of Andalusian descent). All Lipizzaners can be traced back to six stallions from this time: Pluto (Fredericksborg), Conversano and Neapolitano (Neapolitan), Favory and Maestoso (Kladruber), and Siglavy (Arab).

THE CAPRIOLE

The movement known as the Capriole, which is performed by the Spanish Riding School, is the ultimate expression of co-operation between horse and rider. From a standstill, the horse jumps vertically in the air to a height of about 1.8 m (6 ft), kicks out its hind feet, and lands back on the spot where it took off. In battle, this maneuver was used to escape when horse and rider were encircled by enemies.

Later attempts at crossing with other blood, such as Thoroughbred and Anglo-Arab, were not very successful, and the Andalusian has always remained the most important line.

When the Austro-Hungarian stud was broken up in 1918, the Lipizza stud was relocated in Italy, and the quality of the horses there was allowed to deteriorate. However, after World War II, Lipizza became part of Yugoslavia, new stock was imported, and the breed is now flourishing there again.

THE SPANISH RIDING SCHOOL

The Spanish Riding School of Vienna was originally founded in 1758 to educate the nobility in the art of horsemanship. Lipizzaners are now the only breed used there, but in the early days other types, such as spotted horses, were also used. Only stallions are used in the school. Lipizzaners mature late, and they begin their training at four years old. Several years' training are needed to teach a horse the advanced movements seen in the School's displays. All the movements demonstrated in the displays are based on natural movements seen in young horses at play, and were originally developed as battle maneuvers to avoid or fend off an attacking enemy.

The Spanish Riding School's stud, founded in 1798, is now at Piber in southern Austria. Stallions standing there must have excelled in the School, and the mares are also put through performance tests, to ensure that the highest standards are maintained.

Foals of gray parents are born black, and turn gray by the time they are about seven years old. At an early age they show the presence of the breed.

The Lipizzaner is intelligent and docile, and as well as being an excellent school and driving horse, it also makes a good riding horse.

The Lipizzaner is also bred in Hungary, where some are crossed with trotters to produce outstanding driving horses that have been very successful in Combined Driving competitions.

KEY FACTS

Color: gray; born dark and lighten as they mature.
Height: 15–16 hands.
Physique: largish head with straight profile, small ears, crested neck, compact body, powerful rounded hindquarters, strong clean legs.
Character: intelligent, obedient, willing.
Principal uses: high-school dressage, driving.

ANCESTRY

Arab
Barb
Andalusian
Neapolitan
Kladruber
Fredericksborg

Lipizzaner

HAFLINGER

THE HAFLINGER IS the native pony of the Austrian Tyrol. Small Arab horses taken there from Italy are thought to have bred with the native mountain ponies to create the foundation stock for the breed.

The first record of the breed was made in 1868 when an Arab stallion called El Bedavi XXII was used to upgrade the local stock. All members of the breed today can be traced back to him. His son, 249 Folie, who had the typical coloring of the breed, became the foundation sire.

The Haflinger was ideal for pack and transport work in the mountains, and developed into a robust and surefooted animal. It is still used by the Austrian farmers for transporting hay. In addition, it makes a good riding and harness pony.

The Austrian state monitors the breeding of Haflingers, and its numbers are on the increase. It is still reared in the mountains, and animals are allowed to mature until the age of four before being broken in. It is also remarkably long-lived; some Haflingers are said to have worked until at least 40 years of age.

The Avelignese of northern Italy is descended from the same native stock as the Haflinger, and is popular for pack-work in the mountains.

KEY FACTS

Color: chestnut with flaxen mane and tail.
Height: 14 hands.
Physique: medium-sized head with pointed muzzle, strong neck, deep girth, long broad back, well-muscled hindquarters, short legs.
Character: hard-working, docile, frugal.
Principal uses: mountain-work, harness-work, riding.

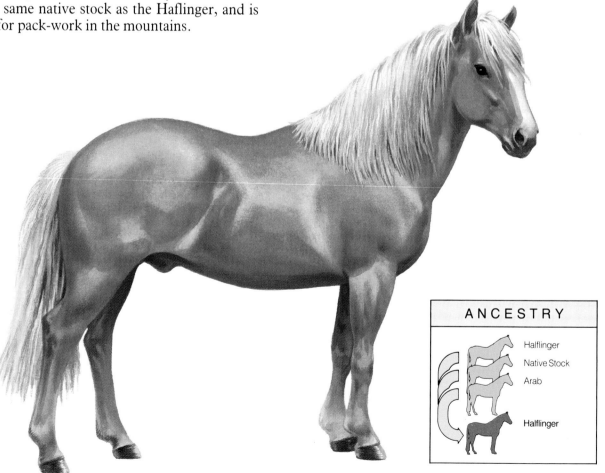

ANCESTRY

Halflinger
Native Stock
Arab

Halflinger

GELDERLAND

THE GELDERLAND COMES from the Dutch province of Gelder, and has been developed from many different European breeds.

It was originally created from crosses of native horses with Andalusians and Norfolk Trotters to produce a versatile farm horse suitable for draft-work, carriage-work and riding. During the 20th century, as the demand has declined for horses for agricultural work, the Gelderland has been crossed with the Oldenburg, Anglo-Norman, East Friesian and Hackney to produce a lighter carriage and riding horse. Considerable work has been put into developing and fixing the type of the new breed.

With its quiet temperament, presence, good conformation and high-stepping action, the Gelderland makes a first-class carriage-horse, and is very popular at shows in the Netherlands. It is used as foundation stock for the Dutch Warm-blood, and it has also had some success as a show-jumper.

KEY FACTS

Color: solid colors; chestnut or gray most common.
Height: 15.2–16 hands.
Physique: plain head with convex profile, strong arched neck, deep shoulder, compact body, powerful hindquarters, high-set tail, short legs.
Character: quiet, good-natured, active.
Principal uses: driving, riding.

ANCESTRY

Native Stock
Andalusian
Norfolk Trotter
Oldenburg
Anglo-Norman
East Friesian
Hackney

Gelderland

SWEDISH WARM-BLOOD

THE EARLIEST TRACES of horses having existed in Sweden date back to 2300 BC. However, there is not enough evidence to indicate what type of horse they were. The Swedish Warm-blood (also known as the Swedish Half-Bred) was first developed some 300 years ago, to provide a good cavalry horse. Imported Oriental (ie, Barb and Arab), Andalusian and Frie-sian stallions were crossed with local native mares. The breed was subsequently built up using Thoroughbred, Trakehner and Hanoverian stallions.

In 1894 the stud book for the breed was opened. All stallions were, and still are, put through rigorous tests for conformation, character and performance before being allowed to breed. They are also tested for their ability at show-jumping, cross-country, dressage and harness-work.

This strict selection procedure has led to the development of one of the very best breeds of sports horse in the world today. It is a powerful, athletic horse, with good conformation and a straight, extravagant action. It excels in show-jumping, eventing and dressage. It has been so successful that only Swedish Warm-Blood horses are used in the Swedish Olympic team, and it has won medals in all three competition disciplines. It is now in demand all over the world.

KEY FACTS

Color: any solid color.
Height: 15.2–16.3 hands.
Physique: small head with elegant features, medium-length neck, strong deep shoulders, deep body, straight back, rounded hindquarters, fine legs with short cannon bones.
Character: intelligent, obedient, sensible, bold,
Principal uses: riding, driving.

ANCESTRY

Arab
Barb
Andalusian
Friesian
Native Stock
Thoroughbred
Trakehner
Hanoverian

Swedish Half-Bred

SWEDISH ARDENNES

THE SWEDISH ARDENNES was developed during the 19th century by crossing imported Ardennes (a heavy draft breed from Belgium and northern France) with the indigenous North Swedish horse, a light draft type with a lively temperament, descended from an ancient Scandinavian strain.

The climate and conditions of the Swedish lowlands are similar to that of the Ardennes region, and the two breeds remained similar in type. Those that were bred in the colder hill-country, however, became smaller and more agile.

The Swedish Ardennes was originally developed to provide a heavy draft horse for working the land. It can withstand extreme variations in climate, it is very strong, is an exceptionally eager worker, and can survive on frugal keep. As there is now little demand for it for agricultural work its numbers are declining, although it is still used for hauling timber in mountain areas that are inaccessible to machinery.

KEY FACTS

Color: black, brown, bay, chestnut.
Height: 15.2–16 hands.
Physique: small head, crested neck, immensely muscular compact body, short legs, little feathering.
Character: docile, kind, gentle, energetic.
Principal uses: draft.

ANCESTRY

Ardennes
Swedish Horse

Swedish Ardennes

FREDERICKSBORG

THE FREDERICKSBORG is the oldest, and was for a long time the most important, horse breed in Denmark. It was established at the Royal Fredericksborg Stud founded in 1562 by King Frederick II, and was named after him.

Andalusians and Neapolitans were used as foundation stock. The resulting breed was considered to be the best of all at the high-school equitation which was so popular in the courts of Europe from the 16th to 18th century. In addition, it was good in harness.

The Stud supplied Fredericksborgs to all the courts of Europe, and it was also popular for improving other breeds – including even the Lipizzaner. The breed was so much in demand that by the early 19th century its quality had declined, and by 1839 there were so few Fredericksborgs left there that the Fredericksborg Stud was closed. The remaining stock was used to keep the breed going, but it has had to be built up using imported blood. In 1923 Fredericksborgs began to be registered again, but even today its numbers are not great.

The purebred Fredericksborg is a very strong horse that is good in harness and for light draft work. Attempts have been made to lighten it to make is more suitable for general riding.

KEY FACTS

Color: chestnut most common.
Height: 15.2–16 hands.
Physique: large plain head, strong neck, powerful shoulders, deep chest, long strong body, straight croup, strong legs.
Character: good-tempered, active, tractable.
Principal uses: harness, riding.

ANCESTRY

Andalusian

Neapolitan

Fredericksborg

KNABSTRUP

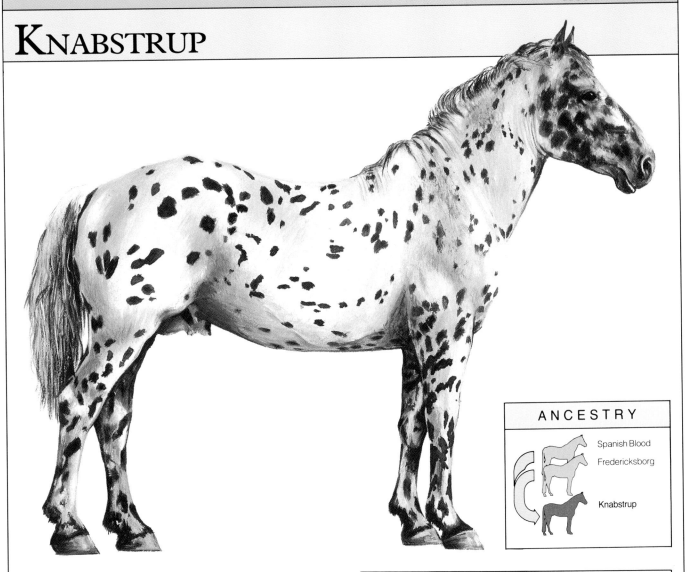

ANCESTRY

Spanish Blood

Fredericksborg

Knabstrup

THE KNABSTRUP is a spotted horse from Denmark that dates back to the time of the Napoleonic wars. A spotted mare of Spanish origins named Flaebehoppen was brought to Denmark and crossed with a palomino Fredericksborg stallion. Their progeny, a spotted stallion named Flaebehingsten, became the foundation sire of the breed. As with the Appaloosa, the patterning varies from horse to horse, and no two are the same.

The Knabstrup became very popular, but unfortunately it has been bred for pattern at the expense of conformation, and as a result the type now varies considerably. At its best it is very similar to the Fredericksborg, but with a lighter build.

It is much in demand in the circus-ring, but is also a good general riding horse.

KEY FACTS

Color: spotted; Appaloosa patterns on a roan base.
Height: 15.3 hands.
Physique: similar to but lighter than the Fredericksborg.
Character: intelligent, tractable, active.
Principal uses: riding, circus.

DØLE

THE DØLE IS AN ANCIENT BREED that originates from the Gudbransdal Valley between Oslo and the North Sea coast in Norway. It is the most widespread of the Norwegian breeds, accounting for about two-thirds of its total equine population.

It is similar in type and appearance to the Friesian horse and the Dale and Fell ponies. This might be due to their being descended from the same pre-historic stock. However, it is more likely that cross-breeding between indigenous breeds occurred when Friesian merchants took their horses to both Norway and England during the 5th to 9th centuries. However, there are no records to verify this.

The Døle varies in size due to the fact that some have been crossed with heavy draft breeds to produce a heavy working horse, while others have been crossed with Thoroughbreds to produce a lighter type. This variety of type means that Døles can be found for heavy draft, lumber and agricultural work, general harness-work, and for riding.

An offshoot of the Døle, the Døle Trotter, was created in the 19th century by crossing the Døle with Thoroughbred blood to produce a fast, active harness horse. It is now used for racing.

KEY FACTS

Color: solid colors, usually black, brown or bay.
Height: 14.2–15.2 hands.
Physique: varies from draught type to lighter pony type; small head, crested neck, strong shoulders, deep girth, powerful hindquarters, short legs, moderate feathering.
Character: tough, adaptable, active.
Principal uses: draft, riding, harness.

ANCESTRY

Native Stock
Thoroughbred
Danish Draft Breeds
Dole

FJORD

THE NORWEGIAN FJORD PONY is an ancient and primitive breed. It is probably descended from the Asiatic wild horse which is depicted in prehistoric cave paintings and which it still closely resembles. Its upright mane suggests that it developed in a land where it did not have to contend with the rain.

The Fjord was the mount of the Vikings, who used it for horse-fights. The Vikings were also the first people to use a pony to pull a plow. In addition, it may have been the Fjord that they took to Iceland, and which provided the foundation stock for the Icelandic pony. Very little cross-breeding has taken place since that time, and the Fjord has probably changed little.

Selective breeding has produced a pony that is robust, hard-working and frugal. It is also long-lived and very fertile. In addition, it has a kind, gentle nature and is very sociable. It is still indispensable in mountain areas that are inaccessible to tractors and lorries, where it is used for farm-work, pack-work, in harness and for riding. And it has been exported to other Scandinavian countries that have no native ponies, and to Germany.

The Fjord's popularity is not just as a working pony, however. It is widespread throughout Norway as a children's pony, and for competition driving.

KEY FACTS

Color: yellow or mouse dun with pronounced dorsal stripe, silver and black mane and tail.
Height: 13–14.2 hands.
Physique: concave profile, coarse upright mane, short neck merging into shoulder with no definition, powerful body, short legs, some feathering.
Character: tireless, tractable.
Principal uses: pack-work, farm-work, harness.

ANCESTRY

Asiatic Wild Horse

Norwegian Fjord Pony

FINNISH

KEY FACTS

Color: chestnut, bay, brown, black.
Height: 15.2 hands.
Physique: medium-sized head, short neck, upright shoulder, deep chest, long back, strong hindquarters, strong legs with light feathering.
Character: quiet, docile, tractable, lively, intelligent.
Principal uses: farm-work, riding, trotting races.

THE FINNISH IS an amalgamation of the Finnish Universal and the Finnish Draft. These two breeds were derived from various imported breeds of draft horses that were crossed with the indigenous forest pony.

The Finnish stud book was established in 1907 and from that time the breed has been selectively bred. Finland has always developed horses on the basis of performance rather than looks or breeding, and all stallions are put through performance tests before being allowed to breed. The breed has strength, speed, stamina, agility and endurance and is good natured. It is easy to train, and is also lively and intelligent. There are heavier and lighter versions of the breed, and it is used as a general all-rounder, for working the land and hauling timber, for general draft work, in harness and for riding.

The Finnish is also an excellent trotter, and many farmers enter their horses in local trotting races. In fact, a light version of the Finnish is now being bred specifically for this purpose.

ANCESTRY

Indigenous
Forest Pony

Finnish Draft

Finnish

ICELANDIC

THE ICELANDIC PONY is based on stock taken to Iceland by the Vikings when they colonized it between AD 870 and AD 930, and probably included the Fjord pony and a group of ponies from the Lotofen islands. Later, settlers from Scotland, the Orkneys and Shetland brought their own ponies. These have blended into one breed, but various types and sizes can still be seen.

Many centuries of isolated breeding by natural selection in harsh and rugged conditions has produced ponies that are tough, agile, strong, surefooted, and full of stamina.

The Icelandic has always been invaluable to the Icelanders, and is still bred in large numbers. It is used as a pack-horse, for transport, communications, agricultural work and riding, as well as for meat. A useful feature of the breed is that on a one-way trip it can always be relied upon to find its own way home.

A distinctive feature of the breed is that in addition to the walk, trot and canter, most ponies have two very easy and comfortable riding gaits, the amble and the tölt. The amble is a running walk; the tölt is a very rapid version of the amble which can increase to the speed of a canter. The tölt is particularly valuable for travelling fast across steep, icy terrain, and ponies with this gait are much in demand.

KEY FACTS

Color: most colors.
Height: 12–13 hands.
Physique: large head, short strong neck, deep compact body, strong clean legs, large feet, thick mane and tail.
Character: docile, friendly, independent.
Principal uses: draft, transport, farm-work, riding.

ANCESTRY

Fjord
Celtic Pony

Icelandic

SALERNO

ANCESTRY

Neapolitan
Andalusian

Salerno

ITALY WAS ONE OF the first areas in the world where horses were bred; the Etruscans are known to have bred horses there 2,500 years ago. Ever since, horse-breeding has played an important part in the life of the country, and in the Salerno they produced a top-class riding horse.

The Salerno was developed during the 16th century in the Salerno area near Naples. It evolved from cross-breeding between Andalusians and Neapolitans (a cross between Barb, Arab and Spanish stock, and now extinct).

The Salerno was popular with the Italian army, and it is now used as a general riding horse. Although its numbers are on the decline it is playing an important part in the creation of the new Italian Saddle-Horse. The Italian Saddle-Horse is being developed by crossing and upgrading the regional Italian saddle-horse breeds to produce a good general riding and competition horse.

KEY FACTS

Color: any solid color.
Height: 16 hands.
Physique: large refined head, good shoulders, prominent withers, strong sloping hindquarters, short legs.
Character: intelligent, responsive.
Principal uses: riding, cross-breeding.

ITALIAN HEAVY DRAFT

ANCESTRY

Breton

Italian Heavy Draft

KEY FACTS

18
16
14
12
10
8
6

0

Color: liver chestnut with flaxen mane and tail.
Height: 15–16 hands.
Physique: fine long head, short crested neck, powerful shoulders, deep broad chest, robust body with broad flat back, round hindquarters, muscular legs, some feathering.
Character: lively, docile.
Principal uses: agricultural work, meat.

THE ITALIAN HEAVY DRAFT was created in the 19th century in northern and central Italy. Thoroughbred, Hackney and Arab stallions were crossed with local mares to produce a fast, active working horse. However, the strongest influence on the breed was the Breton, with which it was crossed during the early 20th century to produce a heavier, more powerful horse.

Its speed, energy and willingness to work made it invaluable to Italian farmers before the days of mechanization. Today there is little demand for it for this type of work; its numbers are dwindling and it is kept mainly for meat.

ANDALUSIAN

THE ANDALUSIAN, from the Andalusia region of southern Spain, has always been one of the most famous and sought-after breeds in Europe.

Its origins are unclear. Some people insist that it is a pure-bred native horse. Others believe that it developed through crosses of the native Andalusian horses, light agile animals probably descended from the Barb, with Arabs and Barbs brought to Spain by the Moors in the 8th century.

The Andalusian type was an ideal cavalry horse due to its ability at high-school work. (The movements performed today by the Spanish Riding School of Vienna are all based on maneuvers that horses were required to perform in battle.) Demonstrations of high-school work were popular among the nobility of Europe, and from the 15th to the 18th century the Andalusian was used to found many other breeds – the Lipizzaner in Austria, the Kladruber in Bohemia (now Czechoslovakia), and the Altér Real and Lusitano in Portugal. At one time it was in such demand that the exportation of breeding

KEY FACTS

Color: usually gray.
Height: 15.2–16 hands.
Physique: broad forehead, large eyes, convex profile, long arched neck, deep short body, powerful rounded hindquarters, strong legs with short cannon bone, luxuriant mane and tail.
Character: docile, calm, willing, proud, agile.
Principal uses: high-school, parades, bull-fighting.

Below: *This Andalusian displays all the presence and beauty for which the breed is renowned. For several centuries the Andalusian was the premier riding horse in Europe.*

Right: *Andalusians being driven four-in-hand. It is less commonly seen in this role than as a saddle-horse.*

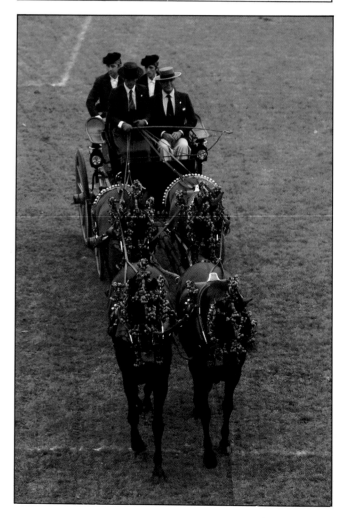

stock was banned on pain of death.

By the early 19th century, however, the breed's survival was in jeopardy. During the reign of Philip III of Spain, it had been crossed with several other breeds to make it heavier. During the Peninsular War (1808–14), Napoleon's marshals took the best of the stock, and many strains were wiped out. The breed's survival at this time was due to the Carthusian monks in the monasteries of Jerez, Seville and Castello, who had been breeding Andalusians since the 15th century with great devotion and attention to purity of line. These escaped the twin ravages of cross-breeding and the Napoleonic wars. A new stud was founded and the breed began to flourish once more.

The Andalusian's influence was not confined to Europe. Many were taken to the New World by the Conquistadores, where they gradually spread throughout North and South America. In the United States the Appaloosa, the Quarter-Horse, the Saddlebred and the Mustang all have Andalusian ancestors, as do the Peruvian Paso, the Paso Fino of Puerto Rico, and the Criollo of Argentina. The Andalusian's inborn *paso* gait, a disjointed four-beat gait, was developed to great practical effect in the Peruvian Paso and the Paso Fino.

In Spain today, the pure-bred Andalusian is a great luxury. It is usually only ridden on special occasions: in street parades, in demonstrations of high-school dressage, and as the mount of the *rejoneadores* (the mounted bull-fighters).

The Andalusian has an excellent temperament. It is intelligent, docile, calm and easy to work with. In motion it is elegant and animated. With its spectacular, high-stepping, dishing action, swinging its forelegs wide to the side as it moves, it is the center of attention whenever it appears.

ANCESTRY

Native Stock
Barb
Arab

Andalusian

ALTÉR REAL

THE ALTÉR REAL is the national horse of Portugal. It was founded from the Andalusian, which it resembles quite closely.

During the 18th century, demonstrations of high-school equitation were popular amongst the courts of Europe, and in 1747 the Portuguese Royal Stud was founded in the Alentego Province to breed suitable horses. About 300 Andalusian mares were imported from Spain to provide foundation stock. The intelligent, athletic horses that were bred there were well suited to the demands of high school.

At the beginning of the 19th century, during the reign of Napoleon, the breed's numbers were drastically reduced. High school had by this time gone out of fashion, and for several decades Altérs were crossed with Thoroughbred, Arab, Norman and Hanoverian blood, with the result that the breed's quality declined quite drastically.

By the early 20th century, however, the Altér's qualities were beginning to be appreciated again, and measures were taken to re-establish it by crossing pure Altérs with Andalusians.

Since 1932, the Portuguese government has supported the re-development of the breed through a program of selective breeding. This has resulted in a riding horse of great quality and elegance. Its intelligence, powerful physique, and high-stepping action also make it well suited to displays of high-school dressage.

KEY FACTS

Color: bay, brown or gray.
Height: 15–16 hands.
Physique: medium-sized head, convex profile, strong shoulders, deep broad chest, short body, powerful hindquarters, hard legs, flexible hocks.
Character: intelligent, temperamental, brave.
Principal use: riding.

ANCESTRY

Andalusian

Altér Real

LUSITANO

KEY FACTS

Color: usually gray; can be any solid color.
Height: 15–16 hands.
Physique: small head, straight profile, small ears, muscular neck, compact body, powerful hindquarters, long fine legs, abundant mane and tail.
Character: intelligent, responsive, very brave.
Principal uses: riding, bull-fighting.

THE LUSITANO, like the Altér Real, is descended from the Andalusian, but is an altogether tougher horse. It is similar to the Andalusian, but has more Arab blood.

At one time it was used by the Portuguese cavalry; and, owing to its great strength, it was popular with farmers as a light draft and riding horse.

However, it is as the mount of the *rejoneadores* (mounted bull-fighters) of the Portuguese bull-ring that it is now famous. Like other horses of Andalusian descent, it has a high-stepping action and powerful hindquarters, and is easily trained in the type of high-school work that is required for bull-fighting. The fastest and most agile Lusitanos are used in the actual fight, and as it is considered a disgrace for a horse to be touched by a bull its agility, skill, speed, obedience and great courage are tested to the full.

ANCESTRY

Andalusian

Arab

Lusitano

SKYROS

IN CLASSICAL TIMES Greece was famous for its horses and horsemen. Today, however, it only has a few breeds of native pony. Of these the Skyros, from the island of Skyros, is both the best known and the smallest, the other better-known breeds being the Pindos and the Peneia.

The Skyros, an ancient pony whose origins can be traced back to the Tarpan, is finely built. On its native island it has always been used as a jack-of-all-trades, for pack-work and light farm-work, for transporting water, and for riding. On the mainland, it is more often used as a children's riding pony.

KEY FACTS

Color: dun, brown, gray.
Height: 9.1–11 hands.
Physique: small head and ears, short neck, upright shoulders, narrow body, long legs, tendency towards cow hocks.
Character: hard-working.
Principal uses: pack-work, farm-work, children's riding pony.

ANCESTRY

Tarpan

Skyros

BOSNIAN

THE BOSNIAN is a native of the mountain areas of Bosnia and Herzegovina, in Yugoslavia, although today it is bred in large numbers all over the Balkans. It is of ancient lineage, being descended from the wild Tarpan pony, and has been improved by crossing with Arab blood.

It shows all the characteristics of good mountain pony breeds. It is intelligent, hardy, surefooted, strong and has great powers of endurance. The government recognizes its value for farm-work and pack-work in modern Yugoslavia, and it is selectively bred in state studs. Only stallions that have passed an endurance test, consisting of carrying a heavy load for 10 miles (16 km), are allowed to breed. It is currently being bred to increase the size.

There is still great demand for the Bosnian. In addition to being a good working pony, it is also used for riding.

KEY FACTS

Color: dun, brown, chestnut, gray, black.
Height: 12.2–15 hands.
Physique: compact mountain pony; thick mane and tail.
Character: intelligent, enduring.
Principal uses: pack-work, farm-work.

ANCESTRY

Tarpan
Arab
Bosnian

TARPAN

ANCESTRY

Mongolian Wild Horse

Asiatic Wild Horse

Tarpan

THE WILD TARPAN was originally a native of Poland and Russia. Some people have claimed that it was one of the original species of wild horse. However, evidence now suggests that it evolved as a cross between the original Southern horse type of western Asia (the proto-Arab) and the Northern type of north-eastern Europe (which includes the Mongolian Wild Horse, which the Tarpan closely resembles) during the Ice Age.

Those that had been caught and domesticated were used by the peasants as general working ponies. However, Tarpan meat was considered a delicacy, and by the end of the 18th century, it had been hunted nearly to extinction. The last wild Tarpan was reported killed in 1879. The breed has since been "re-created" using domesticated Tarpan-type ponies together with others that had been running free in special reserves set up at the end of the 19th century. Through a process of careful selective breeding many of the wild Tarpan's features have been restored.

Today there is a group of Tarpans roaming the state-run reserve in Popielno forest, Poland, where they are studied by scientists and archeologists.

Many breeds of pony across Europe are directly

KEY FACTS

Color: mouse to brown with dorsal stripe, dark mane and tail, zebra stripes may appear on forelegs and inner thighs.
Height: 13 hands.
Physique: long broad head, short thick neck, sloping shoulders, long back, thin hindquarters, fine legs.
Character: intractable, tenacious.
Principal uses: zoo exhibit, research; also roams wild.

descended from the Tarpan, and still resemble it closely, including the Gotland, Norway's only native breed, the Huzul of Poland, and the Karabar from the USSR.

KONIK

THE KONIK IS DIRECTLY descended from the Tarpan. The subsequent addition of Arab blood has refined its appearance, accounting for its name which means "little horse." It has been bred in Poland for many centuries and has influenced the development of many other Polish and Russian breeds. Today it is bred at several national stud farms as well as by local farmers.

The Konik is tough, robust and a frugal feeder; it is also good-natured, willing and easy to handle. It has always been popular with Polish farmers as a general working pony, and also makes a good children's riding pony.

It takes a long time to mature, but has an exceptionally long life-span, and is very fertile.

KEY FACTS

Color: yellow, blue or gray dun, usually with dorsal stripe.
Height: 13.1 hands.
Physique: large head, well-proportioned body, tendency to cow hocks.
Character: good-natured, tough, willing.
Principal uses: farm-work, riding.

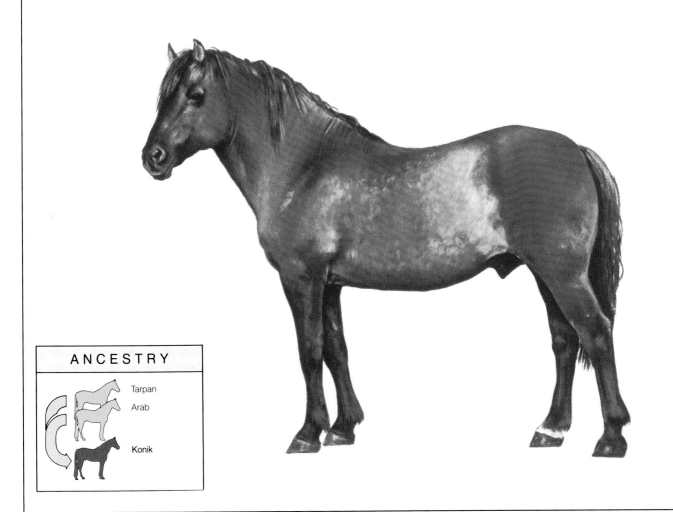

ANCESTRY

Tarpan
Arab
Konik

WIELKOPOLSKI

ANCESTRY

Trakehner
Hanoverian
Thoroughbred
Konik
Poznan
Masuren
East Prussian

Wielkopolski

THE WIELKOPOLSKI of Poland has been created by amalgamating the old Masuren and Poznan breeds.

The Masuren was a continuation of the Trakehner breed. It was bred from horses left behind at the Trakehnen stud (formerly in East Prussia) at the end of World War II. It was bred there with great care, following the principles laid down for the Trakehner breed. The Poznan was another breed based on Trakehner stock. These two breeds were extensively cross-bred, and they have now been combined into one stud book under the new breed name of Wielkopolski.

Poland has a total of 42 major stud farms, and the Wielkopolski is bred at 13 of them. All stallions must pass both conformation checks and performance tests. They also continue to work either under saddle or in harness. This careful program of selective breeding is resulting in an increase in the size and quality of the Wielkopolski.

The Wielkopolski makes a good all-rounder. It is used for light draft work on some farms, and also makes a good general riding horse. It is also proving itself as a competition horse, and this aspect of the breed is being specifically developed.

KEY FACTS

Color: chestnut or bay most common.
Height: 16 hands.
Physique: small head, strong neck, deep girth, medium-length back, good hindquarters, fine legs.
Character: gentle, intelligent, active.
Principal uses: riding, farm-work.

KLADRUBER

KEY FACTS

Color: gray; sometimes black.
Height: 16–17 hands.
Physique: Andalusian type but larger: convex profile, strong arched neck, long body, rounded hindquarters.
Character: proud, intelligent, obedient, good-natured.
Principal uses: driving, riding.

THE KLADRUBY STUD in Czechoslovakia is the oldest operational stud farm in the world. It was founded by Emperor Maximilian II in 1597, and is the home of the Kladruber breed. The Kladruber is closely related to the Lipizzaner, both being directly descended from the Andalusian, but is a taller and heavier horse.

Maximilian imported Andalusians from Spain and created a new breed that had great purity of line, the only other blood being Lipizzaner from the Lipizza stud, and possibly Barb and Neapolitan. The Kladruber was bred specifically as a ceremonial coach-horse, particularly for use at the Imperial Court in Vienna.

The Kladruber's numbers had become seriously depleted by the end of World War II, and Anglo-Norman, Hanoverian and Oldenburg blood have been used to rebuild the breed. Today gray Kladrubers are still bred at the Kladruby Stud, while black Kladrubers are bred at the nearby Slatinany Stud.

Although the Kladruber is used for riding, it has the perfect temperament for a coach-horse, being obedient, good-natured, proud and intelligent, and it is in this area that it excels. It is seen in marathon driving competitions; and demonstrations of Kladrubers driven 16-in-hand are popular features at international shows.

ANCESTRY

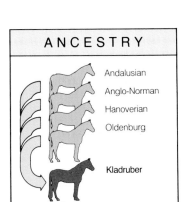

Andalusian

Anglo-Norman

Hanoverian

Oldenburg

Kladruber

SHAGYA ARAB

THE SHAGYA ARAB was developed at the Babolna Stud in Hungary (now in the Ukraine) from about the 1830s. A group of Arab stallions and mares was imported from the desert and crossed with native Babolna stock. One of these stallions, a gray called Shagya, was a sire of great potency, and became the foundation sire of the breed. Careful selective breeding has led to the development of a specific type of Arab that is more robust than the pure-bred Arab.

The Shagya became known as a good cavalry and light carriage-horse, although it was also used for light draft-work and general riding. It was soon in demand in central and eastern Europe, and is still bred in these countries as well as in Germany and the United States.

The Shagya makes a good general riding and competition horse. It is tough and athletic, and can thrive on poor keep.

KEY FACTS

Color: usually gray.
Height: 15 hands.
Physique: Arab type but a little more robust.
Character: intelligent, good-natured, enduring.
Principal uses: cavalry, riding, driving.

ANCESTRY

Syrian Arab

Shagya Arab

FURIOSO

HUNGARY HAS ALWAYS excelled at producing high-quality horses through its stud system. The Furioso is one of several Hungarian half-breds, the others being the Gidran, Kisber and North Star. These horses have always excelled as harness-horses and now are highly successful in driving competitions. They have been exported all over the world.

The Furioso was established in the mid-19th century by crossing native Hungarian mares, which were small and fast, with plenty of stamina, with Thoroughbreds and Arabs. The foundation sire was an English Thoroughbred called Furioso, foaled in 1836, from which the breed takes its name.

The Furioso is an elegant and versatile horse, and is well suited for general and competition riding as well as for driving. It has been successful in the three areas of show-jumping, eventing and dressage; and in harness displays style and endurance.

The Furioso is now crossed extensively with the North Star breed (created by crossing Thorough-breds with native mares) to produce the Mezo-hegyes, which is fast becoming Hungary's premier sports horse.

KEY FACTS

Color: dark colors; often has white markings.
Height: 16 hands.
Physique: long strong neck, powerful shoulders, long strong back, powerful hindquarters, low-set tail.
Character: robust, intelligent, tractable.
Principal uses: riding, driving.

ANCESTRY

Thoroughbred
Arab
Native Stock

Furioso

MURAKOSI

THE MURAKOSI IS Hungary's draft horse, and comes from the area around the River Mura in the south of the country. It was developed during the late 19th and early 20th centuries, when there was great demand for a strong, fast draft horse.

It was created by crossing native Hungarian mares, known as Mur-Insulan, with Percherons, Ardennes, Norikers and Hungarian half-breds (which contained Thoroughbred and Arab blood). This produced a very strong and active draft horse that was ideal for heavy farm-work. It was also used by the army.

The Murakosi was so popular that, after World War I, one in every five horses in Hungary was a member of the breed. However, many were killed in World War II, and now that it is no longer much in demand for farm-work, its numbers are not likely to increase again.

KEY FACTS

Color: chestnut with flaxen mane and tail.
Height: 16 hands.
Physique: large head with convex profile, strong frame, pronounced dip in back, powerful hindquarters, muscular legs with light feathering.
Character: kind, willing, active.
Principal uses: agricultural, draught-work.

ANCESTRY

Native Stock
Ardennes
Percheron
Noriker
Hungarian Half-Bred

Murakosi

ORLOV TROTTER

ANCESTRY

Danish Blood
Arab
Dutch Blood
Thoroughbred
Mecklenburg
Norfolk Trotter

Orlov Trotter

KEY FACTS

Color: usually gray or black.
Height: 15.2–17 hands.
Physique: small head, long neck, upright shoulder, broad chest, deep girth, long straight back, powerful loins, muscular hindquarters, fine hard legs with some feathering.
Character: active, bold.
Principal uses: trotting, harness, riding.

THE ORLOV TROTTER is probably the best known of the Russian horse breeds. It was developed during the 18th century at a time when trotting races were very popular in Russia.

The breed was the creation of Count Alexius Grigorievich Orlov who in 1777 crossed an Arab stallion, Smetanka, with a mare of Danish origins (probably Fredericksborg). This produced a colt, Polkan, who inherited the bad as well as the good features of his father. In particular his forehand action was poor. However, when crossed with a black Dutch mare, Polkan sired a stallion, Bars 1, who was to become the foundation sire of the breed.

Further crossing with Arab, Thoroughbred, Norfolk Trotter and Mecklenburg blood, together with in-breeding to Polkan, established the breed type, and careful selective breeding further improved it.

During the 19th century, the Orlov Trotter was the best trotting horse in the world. However, it has now been superseded by the American Standardbred. More recently, the Orlov has been crossed with the Standardbred to produce the Russian Trotter.

The Orlov Trotter was also used as the basis for the German Trotter, a breed that has since been improved by crossing with the Standardbred and the French Trotter to produce a small horse with a very long-striding action.

DON

THE DON WAS THE HORSE of the famous Russian Cossacks. It comes from the area around the River Don on the Russian steppes.

Originally the Don was a tough, wiry, light-framed, active, Oriental type based on local stock. It more than proved its worth against Napoleon's retreating army in the winter of 1812. While the French horses died of starvation and exhaustion, the Cossacks mounted on their Dons came back to the attack again and again until they had driven the French out of Russia. And they still had the energy to make the long journey back to Moscow.

During the 19th century the breed was upgraded by crossing with Turkoman, Karabakh and Karabir stallions that were allowed to run free with the Dons. It was further refined by crossing with Thoroughbred and Orlov Trotter blood. The Don became a larger, better looking horse as a result.

The Don has been used to improve the Bashkersky, a versatile and enduring breed from the Bashkiria region of the USSR that is used for riding and pulling sleighs. It has been used to refine the Kazakh, a highly-valued riding pony due to its comfortable, ambling gait. It has been crossed with the old Kirghiz to produce a new breed, the New Kirghiz, an excellent mountain horse. And it is used as foundation stock for the Budyonny.

KEY FACTS

Color: chestnut, bay, gray most common.
Height: 15.2–16.2 hands.
Physique: medium-sized head with wide-set eyes, long neck, long broad back, strong hindquarters, long hard legs.
Character: calm, frugal, great stamina.
Principal uses: riding, endurance riding.

ANCESTRY

Turkoman
Karabakh
Karabair
Thoroughbred
Orlov Trotter

Don

BUDYONNY

THE BUDYONNY is a relatively recent Russian breed, having been created in the early 20th century at the Army Stud at Rostov by a famous cavalry officer, Marshal Budyonny. His intention was to produce a good cavalry horse.

The breed was created by crossing Dons and Thoroughbreds – Thoroughbred stallions on Don mares achieving much better results than the other way round. Kazakh blood was also added. A highly selective breeding program was followed, with all animals being tested for speed, fitness, and endurance. As early as 1948 the breed had been fixed and was breeding to type. It was used for cavalry, harness and draft work. It has since been used to improve other Russian regional breeds.

When the Budyonny was no longer in demand as a cavalry horse, it was re-crossed with Thoroughbred blood to produce a top-quality riding horse. It has good jumping ability, and excels in all areas of equestrian sports. It is also a successful steeple-chaser due to its Thoroughbred blood.

KEY FACTS

Color: chestnut or bay with golden sheen.
Height: 15.2–16 hands.
Physique: small head, strong neck, long sloping shoulders, strong compact body, croup long and rounded, low-set tail, fine hard legs.
Character: calm, intelligent, good-natured.
Principal uses: riding, steeple-chasing.

ANCESTRY

Thoroughbred

Don

Kazakh

Budyonny

AKHAL TEKÉ

KEY FACTS

Color: usually bay or chestnut with a metallic bloom.
Height: 14.2–15.2 hands.
Physique: small elegant head, long thin neck. high sloping shoulder, long back, shallow body, low-set tail, long legs, sparse mane and tail.
Character: obstinate, temperamental, bold.
Principal uses: riding, competition.

THE AKHAL TEKÉ, from the USSR, is a pure breed of very ancient lineage. Its origins are unclear, but it is probably a strain of the Turkoman breed of Iran. There is evidence to suggest that an Akhal Teké type existed as long ago as 500 BC.

The Akhal Teké is a true desert horse. It has always been kept by the nomadic Turkmen tribes of the isolated plains of Central Asia, who took great pride in the quality and purity of their horses. They would have used it primarily as a war-horse.

The Akhal Teké has great stamina, is very fast, resilient, can survive on little food, and can tolerate extremes of temperature. It also has astonishing powers of endurance, as was proved in 1935 when a group of Akhal Tekés trekked 2,672 miles (4,300 km) from Ashkabad to Moscow, a journey which included 225 miles (360 km) of desert, which they crossed in three days without water.

The Akhal Teké has magnificent movement, and in many respects it makes a very good riding horse, but its intractable nature can make it difficult to handle.

The Akhal Teké is closely related to the Iomud, which is also directly descended from the Turkoman. At 14 hands the Iomud is smaller and more compact than the Akhal Teké, but not as fast.

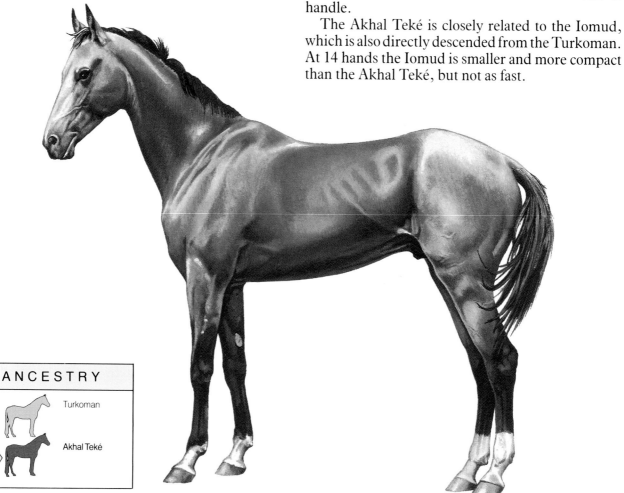

ANCESTRY

Turkoman

Akhal Teké

TERSKY

THE TERSKY IS ANOTHER recent Russian breed. It has been developed at the Tersk stud in the northern Caucasus, originally for the purpose of producing an Arab-type race-horse.

It was founded on the Streletsk Arab, a now extinct large Arab type based on native Ukrainian mares and Oriental stallions. The Streletsk was crossed with Arab-Dons, Thoroughbreds, and Shagyas. The progeny was reinforced with more Arab blood, until in 1948 the Tersky was recognized as a breed.

The intention was to produce a horse that had the speed and endurance of an Arab coupled with the robustness of native stock, for steeple-chasing. Today, however, the Tersky is used for flat-racing. It is not as fast as the Thoroughbred, and is therefore raced against other Arabs.

It is a gentle, elegant, athletic horse with great powers of endurance. Its good movement makes it suitable for dressage. It is also used for endurance riding, and by the army; the beauty and versatility of the breed have also made it popular for the circus-ring. In addition, it has been used to upgrade other Russian breeds.

KEY FACTS

Color: gray most common; can be bay.
Height: 15 hands.
Physique: medium-sized head with straight profile, medium-length neck and back, deep chest, muscular hindquarters, high-set tail, fine hard legs.
Character: gentle, intelligent, enduring.
Principal uses: flat-racing, competition, circus.

ANCESTRY

Streletsk Arab
Kabardin
Don Arab
Shagya Arab
Thoroughbred

Tersky

KARABAKH

ANCESTRY

Persian

Turkoman

Arab

Karabakh

THE KARABAKH is one of the USSR's native mountain horse breeds, and comes from the Karabakh mountains in the region of Azerbaijan. It is a very ancient breed, going back to the 5th century. It contains Turkomen, Persian and Arab blood, and has itself influenced the development of many other Russian breeds, in particular the Don. In the 18th century it became very popular and was exported to many other countries.

It is a light riding horse type, but like all mountain breeds, it is robust, surefooted, quick-witted and calm. There are no pure-bred Karabakhs left, but work is being done to restore the breed.

KEY FACTS

Color: dun, bay or chestnut with a metallic sheen.
Height: 14.2 hands.
Physique: small fine head, strong neck, prominent withers, strong compact body, strong hindquarters, low-set tail, fine legs and good feet.
Character: energetic, calm, robust.
Principal uses: riding.

VLADIMIR HEAVY DRAFT

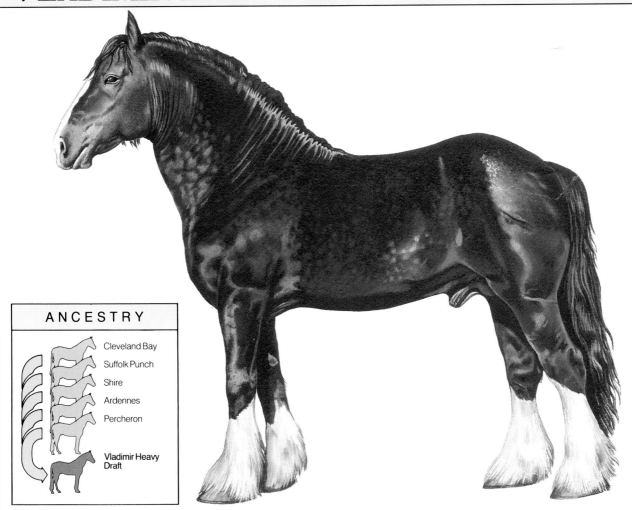

ANCESTRY

Cleveland Bay

Suffolk Punch

Shire

Ardennes

Percheron

Vladimir Heavy Draft

THE VLADIMIR HEAVY DRAFT was founded towards the end of the 19th century in the Vladimir province of the Soviet Union. However, it is now widespread throughout the USSR.

It was developed from the Suffolk Punch and Cleveland Bay, and Ardennes and Percheron blood were also added. From about 1910 until after World War I Shire blood was also added. By 1946 the Vladimir was breeding true and the breed was considered to be fixed. From that time selective breeding using only the best stock has been practiced.

The Vladimir is a horse of great strength. It has good conformation and matures early. It is used for draft-work, and also for pulling troikas.

KEY FACTS

Color: any solid color; bay most common.
Height: 16 hands.
Physique: small head, long strong neck, powerful shoulders, broad medium-length body, stout hindquarters, strong legs with feathering.
Character: docile, good-tempered, active.
Principal uses: draft.

145

BARB

THE BARB IS THE TRADITIONAL mount of the Bedouin tribes of the North African deserts. It takes it name from its native land, the Barbary Coast – now Morocco, Algeria and Libya – where it has lived since prehistoric times.

The Barb is thought to be derived from the wild ancient horse type of northern Europe, unlike the Arab which is derived from the Asiatic type. It is distinguished from the Arab by its ram-like head and broad, straight face and muzzle, its lower-set tail and wilder temperament.

The Barb has played an important part in founding and improving many other breeds. It was taken to Spain in large numbers by the Moors in the 8th century, and was crossed with local mares to produce the Andalusian. While the Turks occupied the eastern Mediterranean and the north coast of Africa, traders from all parts of Europe and Asia acquired Barbs and took them home to be crossed with the local horses. Charles II imported many to improve the speed and stamina of England's early racehorses, and it contributed to the founding of the Thoroughbred.

There are not many pure-bred Barbs left; crossing with the gentler Arab makes them easier to train as riding horses. The Barb has been crossed with the Arab to produce the Libyan Barb, a common breed in North Africa. It is a working horse, and is not selectively bred.

KEY FACTS

18
16
14
12
10
8
6
0

Color: bay, brown, chestnut, black, gray.
Height: 14–15 hands.
Physique: long refined head with straight face, crested neck, flat shoulder, long back with low-set tail, long fine legs.
Character: quick-tempered, tough, courageous.
Principal uses: riding, improving other breeds.

ANCESTRY

European Wild Stock

Barb

CASPIAN

THE CASPIAN IS THOUGHT to be descended from the wild native pony of Iran. This pony, which was actually a miniature horse, was used by the Mesopotamians during the 3rd millennium BC, and it appears in carvings on the walls of Persepolis that date back to the late 6th or early 5th century BC. Since then there have been no records of the pony, and it was thought to have become extinct.

However, in 1965 a group of ponies was discovered on the southern shores of the Caspian Sea in Iran. These ponies, with their distinctive features, bear a striking resemblance to the small horses in the carvings in Persepolis. And further archeological and scientific research has confirmed that the Caspian is indeed directly descended from them. It had survived in an isolated area around the Caspian Sea, and the breed remained pure. It is now thought probable that this ancient pony is the forerunner of the Arab.

The Caspian is fast, has a free, floating action, and has great jumping ability. It is popular both as a children's riding pony, and for competition driving. Its historical importance is appreciated, and although political upheavals have disrupted its

KEY FACTS

Color: bay, brown, chestnut, gray.
Height: 10–12 hands.
Physique: Arab-type head, long neck and shoulder, narrow body with short back, tail set high, fine legs.
Character: gentle, quick-witted.
Principal uses: riding, driving.

breeding in Iran, enough Caspians had been exported to the United States, Britain and Australia to ensure its survival.

ANCESTRY

Asiatic Wild Horse

Caspian

PERSIAN ARAB

ANCESTRY

Asiatic Wild Horse

Persian Arab

DIFFERENT STRAINS OF ARAB have developed which vary slightly from each other in type and size according to climate, pasture, and national preferences. The Persian Arab, raised in a temperate area, is larger and softer than its desert-bred cousins, and does not have the typical "dished" face.

The bones of a horse excavated in western Iran prove that the Arab existed there long before domestication. They also show that the Arab has changed very little since prehistoric times, man having had little influence over its build or appearance.

The Iranians have always claimed that they were the first to domesticate the Arab, and the Persian Arab is one of the oldest pure Arab lines in the world. It has been very carefully maintained through selective breeding and attention to purity of line.

Other strains of Arab in Iran have now been grouped together under the breed name of Plateau Persian. The Plateau Persian was crossed with the Thoroughbred to create the Pahlavan.

KEY FACTS

Color: gray or bay.
Height: 15 hands.
Physique: Arab type but taller; elegant, compact body.
Character: intelligent, lively, kind.
Principal uses: riding, improving other breeds.

BASUTO

Color: chestnut, bay, brown, gray.
Height: 14.2 hands.
Physique: refined head, long neck, straight shoulder, long back, short legs, hard feet.
Character: fearless, enduring.
Principal uses: general riding, trekking.

THE BASUTO PONY comes from Basutoland, South Africa, but is derived from the Cape Horse of the Cape Province.

Traders first imported horses, mostly Arabs and Barbs, into the Cape Province during the 17th century. Further imports of Persian Arabs and Thoroughbreds during the 18th and 19th centuries were crossed with these to produce a tough native horse, the Cape Horse, that was sold in large numbers to the British army in India as cavalry remounts. Around the 1830s, Cape Horses were used in border raids on neighboring Basutoland, and when these were over some were left behind to fend for themselves. As a result of in-breeding, harsh terrain and climate and poor feed, the Cape Horse deteriorated into the Basuto pony. However, the harsh new conditions also made it tough, brave and enduring. It is said to be able to carry a full-grown man up to 80 miles a day.

The Basuto was used in large numbers by the British Army during the Boer Wars. It has been used for polo and racing. It is now in demand all over South Africa as a riding pony, and particularly for trekking.

ANCESTRY

Arab

Barb

Thoroughbred

Persian Arab

Basuto

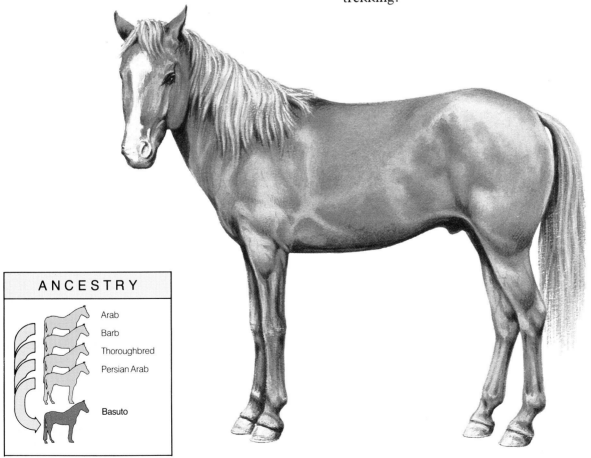

MANIPUR

THE MANIPUR PONY has been bred in the state of Manipur, India, for many centuries. It is derived from the Mongolian wild horse, and has been crossed with Arab blood to improve its conformation and give it more speed.

The Manipur became famous in the 19th century as the original polo pony. Polo had been played in Asia for 2,000 years. Although the game died out in most of India, it continued to be popular in Assam and the Himalayan states. A 7th-century manuscript records polo being played in Manipur on Manipur ponies. In the 1850s, British tea-planters in Assam discovered the game being played on these fast, maneuverable ponies and took it up themselves, spreading its popularity throughout the world.

The Manipur is still used for polo in its homeland, but has been superseded elsewhere by larger, faster horses. It was also reputed to be a good cavalry horse. Being very tough, sturdy, and surefooted, and able to carry heavy loads for long distances, it has always been an invaluable working pony.

KEY FACTS

Color: most colors.
Height: 11–13 hands.
Physique: long head with broad muzzle, deep chest, broad deep body, high-set tail, clean hard legs.
Character: adaptable, lively.
Principal uses: polo, cavalry, general working pony.

ANCESTRY

Mongolian Wild Horse

Arab

Manipur

MONGOLIAN WILD HORSE

The Mongolian Wild Horse (*Equus przewalski poliakov*) is the only surviving truly wild horse, as opposed to those that have escaped from domestication. At one time it was thought to be the basic breed from which all domesticated breeds evolved. Recent evidence suggests, however, that there were four basic groups, and that the Mongolian Wild Horse belonged to the Northern group known as the Primeval Pony.

The Mongolian Wild Horse was discovered in 1881 by Colonel Przewalski roaming the steppes of the Tachin Schara Nuru Mountains (the Mountains of the Yellow Horses), on the western edge of the Gobi desert in Mongolia. The breed is also known as Przewalski's Horse after its discoverer. It has changed little since the Ice Age, due partly to its isolation, and partly to the ferocious temperament of the stallions. Intruders would be seen off long before they got near a herd of mares.

The Mongolian Wild Horse has always been hunted for meat, and it is now nearly extinct although measures are being taken by the Russian and Chinese governments to preserve it. Specimens are kept in zoos around the world.

It has provided the foundation stock for many domesticated breeds, including the Burma pony, the Manipur of India, and the Mongolian pony. The Mongolian pony is one of the oldest domesticated breeds in the world, and was the work pony of the nomadic tribes of Mongolia.

KEY FACTS

Color: dun, usually with mealy muzzle, dorsal stripe, zebra stripes on legs.
Height: 12–14 hands.
Physique: primitive pony type; large head, short upright mane, upright shoulder, broad short body, slight hindquarters, strong legs with short cannon bone.
Character: timid, aggressive, great powers of endurance.

ANCESTRY

Foreign Stock

Asiatic Wild Horse

Mongolian

BURMA

ANCESTRY

Mongolian Wild Horse

Arab

Burma

THE BURMA PONY, sometimes also known as the Shan, has been bred for a long time by the Shan hill-tribes of eastern Burma.

It is closely related to the Manipur, being descended from the Mongolian Wild Horse, but has had more Arab blood added, making it larger.

It is very strong, and has always been used as a working pony. At one time it was also used by the British for playing polo, but it is too slow and unresponsive to be successful in this field.

KEY FACTS

Color: all colors.
Height: 13 hands.
Physique: larger version of the Manipur.
Character: active, adaptable.
Principal uses: all-round working pony.

JAVA

ANCESTRY

Tarpan

Asiatic Wild Horse

Java

INDONESIA'S PONIES are vital to the transport, communications and agriculture of the country, and many of the islands have their own breed. The breeding of many of these ponies is supported by the state. These ponies are generally of primitive type, and over the centuries they have adapted to working in the tropical heat.

The Java is a native of the island of Java and is descended from the Mongolian Wild Horse. As well as being used for general work, it pulls the sados, or two-wheeled taxis, that are used on the island. It is a strong and tireless pony, and willingly pulls a full load all day.

Other island breeds include the Timor, a small, finely-built and very wise pony; the Bali, a very primitive type of pony used for packwork; the Batak from Sumatra, which has been refined and improved by crossing with Arab blood; the Gayoc, also from Sumatra; the Sumbawa, which is very similar to the Sumba; and the Sandalwood, from the islands of Sumba and Sumbawa, a fast, finely-built pony.

KEY FACTS

Color: most colors.
Height: 12.2 hands.
Physique: slightly built, ugly.
Character: willing, tireless.
Principal uses: pulling 2–wheel taxis, all-round work.

SUMBA

Color: dun with dorsal stripe and dark points.
Height: 12.2 hands.
Physique: primitive type, with heavy head and stringy tail.
Character: willing, intelligent, tough.
Principal uses: dancing, all-round work.

THE SUMBA IS A NATIVE of the island of Sumba. It is a primitive type descended from a mixture of the Mongolian Wild Horse and the Tarpan.

It is used for general work on the island, but is most famous as a dancing pony. It is ridden by small boys with no saddle or bridle, and is controlled by someone on foot. It has bells tied to its knees, and dances to a tom-tom rhythm. Its performance is judged on elegance and lightness.

ANCESTRY

Mongolian

Sumba

AUSTRALIAN STOCK HORSE

IN 1971 THE NAME Australian Stock Horse was given to Australia's oldest horse breed, the Waler.

The Waler originally developed from stock brought over from South Africa by the early settlers at the end of the 18th century. These horses were of Spanish, Arab, Barb and Dutch origins, and could have been Cape Horses. They were crossed extensively with Thoroughbred blood from England over the next hundred years to produce a hardy, agile horse that was full of stamina. It was good for stockwork on the big cattle stations, for harness-work and for riding. It was also popular with the British army in India as a cavalry horse.

During the 20th century, more Thoroughbred blood has been added, along with a little Percheron and American Quarter-Horse. The stud book was opened at the time that the breed's name was changed to Australian Stock Horse. Owing to the many influences on the breed conformation varies, and it does not yet breed true to type, although progress is being made towards achieving a uniform breed type. It is a robust Thoroughbred type of horse. It is still used for cattle-work and rodeos, and it also makes a world-class competition horse, particularly in the areas of jumping, eventing and endurance riding.

KEY FACTS

Color: all colors.
Height: 16 hands.
Physique: varies; Thoroughbred type with alert head, deep girth, strong back and hindquarters.
Character: tough, willing, agile.
Principal uses: stock-work, rodeos, general and competitive riding.

ANCESTRY

Arab
Spanish
Thoroughbred
Australian Stock Horse

AUSTRALIAN PONY

ANCESTRY

Arab

Welsh Pony

Exmoor Pony

Shetland Pony

Thoroughbred

Timor Pony

Australian Pony

BRITISH NATIVE PONIES have long been imported into Australia, Welsh ponies and Shetlands being among the most popular.

The Australian pony emerged as a result of crossing some of these breeds with Arab blood to make them lighter and more athletic. The foundation stock was created by crossing Arabs with Welsh ponies, the most famous being a Welsh Mountain Pony stallion called Gray Light, which was imported into Australia in 1911. Subsequently Shetland, Exmoor and Thoroughbred blood were added. By 1929 it had developed as a specific type and a stud book was opened.

The Australian pony combines elegance and character with athleticism, and provides an excellent children's riding pony.

KEY FACTS

Color: all colors.
Height: 12–14 hands.
Physique: Arab-like head, longish neck, sloping shoulders, deep girth, short back, powerful hindquarters, tail set high, short legs, hard feet.
Character: intelligent, lively, enduring.
Principal uses: children's riding pony.

BRUMBY

THE BRUMBY IS A HORSE of the Australian bush that has roamed wild for over 100 years. It is descended from domesticated horses and saddle horses that were turned loose after the gold rush in the mid-19th century.

Only the cleverest and most adaptable horses survived in the harsh conditions of the Australian outback, and the Brumby developed into a tough, wily horse that is very alert. Although the quality of the horses declined due to in-breeding and poor grazing, it flourished in the wild to the point that it was considered a pest, and widespread culling has taken place. It is extremely hard to catch, and difficult to train and ride. However, "Brumby runners" herd the horses into cleverly concealed stockyards and sell the best as saddle horses.

KEY FACTS

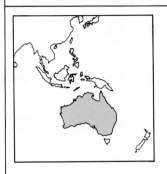

Color: most colors.
Height: varies.
Physique: varies.
Character: intelligent; difficult to catch and train.
Principal uses: too wild for most purposes.

ANCESTRY

Domesticated
Stock and Saddle
Horses

Brumby

INDEX

CREDITS

Quarto would like to thank the following for providing photographs for this publication, and for their permission to reproduce copyright material.

Anne Bazalik
Bridgeman Art Library
Mary Evans Picture Library
Kit Houghton
Bob Langrish
Peter Newark's Military Pictures
Sally-Anne Thompson/Animal Photography

Although we have made every effort to trace and acknowledge all copyright holders, Quarto would like to apologize if there should be any omissions.